# EFFECTIVE INTENTIONS

# Effective Intentions
*The Power of Conscious Will*

ALFRED R. MELE

OXFORD
UNIVERSITY PRESS
2009

# OXFORD
## UNIVERSITY PRESS

Oxford University Press, Inc., publishes works that further
Oxford University's objective of excellence
in research, scholarship, and education.

Oxford  New York

Auckland  Cape Town  Dar es Salaam  Hong Kong  Karachi
Kuala Lumpur  Madrid  Melbourne  Mexico City  Nairobi
New Delhi  Shanghai  Taipei  Toronto

With offices in

Argentina  Austria  Brazil  Chile  Czech Republic  France  Greece
Guatemala  Hungary  Italy  Japan  Poland  Portugal  Singapore
South Korea  Switzerland  Thailand  Turkey  Ukraine  Vietnam

Copyright © 2009 by Oxford University Press, Inc.

Published by Oxford University Press, Inc.
198 Madison Avenue, New York, New York 10016

www.oup.com

Library of Congress Cataloging-in-Publication Data
Mele, Alfred R., 1951–
Effective intentions: the power of conscious will / Alfred R. Mele.
p. cm.
ISBN 978-0-19-538426-0
1. Will.   2. Consciousness.   3. Intentionalism.
I. Title.
BF611.M46   2009
128'.3–dc22      2008038397

2  4  6  8  9  7  5  3

Printed in the United States of America
on acid-free paper

*For Joanna*

# Preface

In November 2007, while I was working on this book, I received the following e-mail message from someone I don't know.

> Dear Dr. Mele,
> I recently purchased a DVD by Dr. Stephen Wolinsky. . . . He explains from the point of neuroscience that there is no such thing as free will, as we can only perceive an action after it has already occurred. Can you please help me with this? I can understand that I don't know what thought will occur next. But that that has already happened is beyond comprehension. Thank you as I am in a lot of despair.

The belief that scientists have proved that there is no such thing as free will is disturbing. (Indeed, there is some evidence that this belief has undesirable effects on behavior; see Vohs and Schooler 2008.) But don't despair. They haven't proved this, as I explain in this book. Nor has anyone proved that there is no such thing as an effective intention, as I also explain.

Effective intentions are (roughly) intentions that issue in corresponding actions. For example, if I have an effective intention to explain this book's title in this preface, it is (roughly) an intention to do that that issues in my doing it. In fact, I do intend to explain the title—especially the subtitle.

The editors of a recent volume titled *Does Consciousness Cause Behavior?* write: "The wide promulgation of two new lines of genuinely scientific...evidence has seized the philosophical and scientific imagination and again brought the whole question [whether consciousness causes behavior] to the forefront of intellectual debate" (Pockett, Banks, and Gallagher 2006, p. 1). They identify Benjamin Libet and Daniel Wegner as the sources of these two new lines of evidence. Wegner's best-known work in this connection is *The Illusion of Conscious Will* (2002), a book that has attracted a great deal of attention. Now, I have a bit of an aversion to using "will" as a noun (except in a legal context), because "will" used in that way is suggestive of the nonnatural and even the supernatural to some readers. Readers who know that I have written a book titled *Free Will and Luck* (2006) may find what I just said surprising. But there I define "free will" as the power or ability to perform free actions, and I treat the concept of free action as the more basic one. ("Free action" has less of a tendency than "free will" to conjure up the supernatural in readers' minds.) In any case, one thing I do in the present book is to examine data and arguments that various scientists and philosophers have offered in support of the illusion thesis about "conscious will" and argue that they leave my thesis—that there are effective intentions—unscathed. My subtitle is intended as a snappy way of signaling some readers—those familiar with work like Wegner's—about an important part of the scientific context of this book.

Portions of this book derive from published work of mine. Parts of chapters 1 and 2 derive from "Conscious Intentions," in Campbell, O'Rourke, and Silverstein (in press). Chapters 3 and 4 incorporate material from chapter 2 of Mele (2006), and section 2 of chapter 4 borrows from a section of Mele (2008a). Parts of chapter 5 derive from Mele (2004) and Mele (2008b). Chapter 6 derives from Mele (2008a). Finally, chapter 8 incorporates some material from

"Free Will: Theories, Analysis, and Data," in Pockett et al. (2006) and Mele (2008b).

Some of the material in this book was presented at a conference on consciousness and free action on Amelia Island, a workshop on free will in Banff, a workshop on Libet's work in Tucson, the Cargèse School on Consciousness, Davidson College, Franklin and Marshall College, the Johann Wolfgang Goethe University, Missouri Western State University, the National Institutes of Health, Simon Fraser University, Stanford University, Syracuse University, Washington State University, and the universities of Birmingham, California–Riverside, Cologne, Edinburgh, Maryland, North Florida, Oxford, Potsdam, Québec à Trois-Rivières, and Sydney. I am grateful to my audiences for their help. For useful feedback on some of the ideas in this book or advice about some of the topics I discuss, I am grateful to students in seminar discussions of an early draft of this book at Florida State University and to John Baer, Bill Banks, Roy Baumeister, Michael Bratman, Peter Carruthers, Randy Clarke, Shaun Gallagher, Peter Gollwitzer, Patrick Haggard, Mark Hallett, Richard Holton, Philipp Hübl, Eddy Nahmias, Sue Pockett, and Tyler Stillman. Neil Levy and Tim Bayne (the latter as a referee) commented on a draft of this book, as did an anonymous referee. I am grateful to them for their guidance.

I completed a draft of this book during my tenure of a 2007–2008 NEH Fellowship and a 2007–2008 sabbatical leave from Florida State University. Any views, findings, conclusions, or recommendations expressed in this book do not necessarily reflect those of the National Endowment for the Humanities. I am grateful to the NEH and FSU for their support.

# Contents

EFFECTIVE INTENTIONS

Occurrent: actually occurring or observable, not potential or hypothetical

ONE

. . .

# Introduction

Some recent scientific claims about human action have created quite a stir. Neuroscientist Benjamin Libet (1985, 2004) contends that the brain decides to initiate actions about a third of a second before the person becomes aware of the decision and that the remaining window of opportunity for free will to get involved is tiny—about 100 milliseconds. Psychologist Daniel Wegner (2002, 2004a, 2008) argues that intentions are not among the causes of corresponding actions. If Wegner is right, then if only beings whose intentions are sometimes among the causes of corresponding actions are capable of acting freely, even Libet's tiny window of opportunity for free will is an illusion.

One of my aims in this book is to show that these striking claims and some related claims about free will, consciousness, and action-production are not warranted by the data. I also show that there is powerful empirical support for the thesis that some conscious intentions are among the causes of corresponding actions. Although I discuss the work of many scientists, my mentioning Libet and Wegner first is no accident. Azim Shariff and coauthors report that "almost all of the works involved in the recent deluge of anti-free will arguments have referenced" Libet's work (Shariff, Schooler, and Vohs 2008, p. 186). And the passage I quoted from Pockett, Banks, and Gallagher (2006) in the Preface locates both Libet and Wegner at center stage in the controversy about human action explored in this book.

1

Scientific evidence is accessible to philosophers, and philosophical argumentation and analysis are accessible to scientists. Even so, some members of each group are dismissive of what the other group has to offer. After writing that "many of the world's leading neuroscientists have not only accepted our findings and interpretations, but have even enthusiastically praised these achievements and their experimental ingenuity" and naming twenty such people, Libet adds: "It is interesting that most of the negative criticism of our findings and their implications have come from philosophers and others with no significant experience in experimental neuroscience of the brain" (2002, p. 292). Later in the article, he writes of one of his critics, "As a philosopher [Gilberto] Gomes exhibits characteristics often found in philosophers. He seems to think one can offer reinterpretations by making unsupported assumptions, offering speculative data that do not exist and constructing hypotheses that are not even testable" (p. 297). (Incidentally, several years ago, when I asked Gomes about his profession, he informed me that he worked in a psychology department.) This is not a one-way street. More than a few philosophers, after hearing a talk of mine on Libet's or Wegner's work, have suggested, on a priori grounds, that they could not have been right anyway. One moral of this book is that this dismissiveness is a mistake—on each side.

In this chapter, I sketch part of a conceptual framework in light of which data such as Libet's and Wegner's can be instructively interpreted and examined. Although this chapter is relatively short, some readers might find themselves wishing it were shorter. For now, I offer such readers two things. The first is a platitude: patience is a virtue. The second is a claim they can test as they read the discussion of empirical work in subsequent chapters: conceptual precision is a virtue, too. In sections 1 and 2, I distinguish among various kinds of intention and describe a way of understanding occurrent intentions that I have developed elsewhere

(Mele 1992). In section 3, drawing on Mele (2003, chap. 9), I provide some background on practical decision making. Section 4 is a preview of this book.

## 1. Occurrent and Standing Intentions

Psychologist Anthony Marcel writes, "Oddly, many psychologists seem to assume that intentions are by their nature conscious" (2003, p. 60). That assumption is the primary topic of chapter 2. A distinction between occurrent and standing intentions is relevant. In this section, I provide a sketch of the distinction and a sketch of an account of occurrent intentions.

I ask myself now, at noon on a Sunday, what I intend to do tomorrow. Reflection on this question may prompt me to form some new intentions, and it may prompt me to recall having formed intentions—that is, having *decided*—to do various things on Monday. (Like many philosophers, I take deciding to A to be an action—specifically, an action of forming an intention to A, as I explain in section 3.[1]) I recall that I decided on Friday to call my travel agent on Monday to book plane tickets for a trip to Corsica and that I decided to reserve a hotel room there once I ordered my tickets. I am now aware that I intend to do these things tomorrow.

Is it possible for me to intend to do these things tomorrow without being aware that this is so? Consider my condition ten minutes before noon—ten minutes before I asked myself about my intentions for tomorrow. Might I have intended then to call my travel agent on Monday—or to fly to Corsica in a couple of months—even though I was not aware of that intention?

I told my father about my intention to fly to Corsica. A day later, he quite properly informed my sister that I intended to fly there without phoning me first to learn whether I was awake, conscious, thinking about Corsica, or anything of the sort. He legitimately attributed the intention to me without supposing that I was conscious of the intention at the time of attribution. In fact, he might have believed that I was sound asleep: he knows my routine, and his conversation with my sister happened after midnight.

The intention my father attributed to me is what I call a *standing intention,* something I analyze elsewhere as a disposition of a certain kind to have corresponding *occurrent* intentions (Mele 2007). Because standing intentions are not at issue in this book, I spare readers the details of the analysis. Proponents of the view that "intentions are by their nature conscious" (if they understand this to entail that we have intentions only when we are conscious of them) may either contend that standing intentions are not actually intentions or assert that their view is about occurrent intentions only.

In Mele (2007), I propose that there are two ways for an intention to *A* to be an *occurrent intention* at a time. One way is for it to be "suitably at work at that time in producing relevant intentional actions or in producing items appropriate for the production of relevant intentional actions"; the other is, roughly, for it to be a conscious intention at that time, provided that the intention "is not wholly constituted by a disposition to have occurrent intentions to *A*" (p. 740). (One way for an intention to fly to Corsica, for example, to be at work is in initiating and sustaining information gathering and reasoning about how to fly there.) These two ways of being an occurrent intention are not mutually exclusive. The same intention may be occurrent in both ways at the same time. This thumbnail sketch of what it is for an intention to be an *occurrent* intention suffices for present purposes. (What it is for an occurrent intention to be an *intention* is discussed shortly.) Readers interested in details suppressed here should consult Mele (2007). On conscious intentions, see chapter 2.

Intentions are a topic of discussion in a variety of fields, including (but definitely not limited to) neuroscience, philosophy, law, and several branches of psychology. It should not be assumed that the term "intention" is understood in the same way in all of these fields. Nor should it be assumed that there is a uniform understanding of the term within each field. Even so, conceptions of intention in different fields sometimes converge, as I am about to illustrate.

Here is a representative account of intention from the neuroscience literature:

> Intention is an early plan for a movement. It specifies the goal of a movement and the type of movement.... We can have intentions without actually acting upon them. Moreover, a neural correlate of intention does not necessarily contain information about the details of a movement, for instance the joint angles, torques, and muscle activations required to make a movement.... Intentions are initially coded in visual coordinates in at least some of the cortical areas within the PPC [posterior parietal cortex]. This encoding is consistent with a more cognitive representation of intentions, specifying the goals of movements rather than the exact muscle activations required to execute the movement. (Andersen and Buneo 2002, p. 191)

This account is similar in some respects to my account of occurrent intentions as executive attitudes toward plans (Mele 1992). In the next several paragraphs, I provide a sketch of my account. What it is for an occurrent intention to be an *intention* is one thing, and what it is for it to be *occurrent* is another. In the remainder of this section, I focus on the former aspect of occurrent intentions.[2]

In my view, plans—which range from simple representations of prospective "basic" actions to complex strategies for achieving remote goals—constitute the representational content of occurrent intentions.[3] In the limiting case, the plan component of an intention has a single "node." It is, for example, a prospective representation I have of raising my right index finger—or a prospective representation of taking a vacation in Lisbon next winter that includes nothing about means to that end nor specific vacation activities. Often, intention-embedded plans are more complex. The intention to check her e-mail that Jan executed this evening incorporated a plan that included clicking on her e-mail icon, typing her password in a certain box, clicking on the OK button, and so on. An agent who successfully executes an occurrent intention is guided by the intention-embedded plan.[4]

Although the contents of intentions are plans, I follow the standard practice of using expressions such as "Jan's intention to check her e-mail now" and "Ken intends to bowl tonight." It should not be inferred from such expressions that the agent's intention-embedded plan has a single node—for example, checking e-mail now or bowling tonight. Often, expressions of an agent's desires and intentions do not identify the full content of the attitude and are not meant to. Jan says, without intending to mislead, "Ken wants to bowl tonight" (or "Ken intends to bowl tonight"), knowing full well that what he wants (or intends) is to bowl with her at MegaLanes tonight for $20 a game until the place closes, as is their normal practice.

I reported that occurrent intentions, in my view, are *executive* attitudes toward plans. According to a popular view of occurrent representational attitudes—for example, Ann's occurrent desire to $A$, Bob's occurrent belief that $p$, Cathy's occurrent desire that $p$, Don's occurrent intention to $A$—one can distinguish between an attitude's representational *content* and its psychological *orientation* (Searle 1983).[5] Orientations include (but are not limited to) believing, desiring, and intending. On my view, the executive dimension of occurrent intentions is intrinsic to the attitudinal orientation *intending*. We can have a variety of attitudes toward plans: for example, we might admire plan $x$, be disgusted by plan $y$, and desire to execute plan $z$. To have the intending attitude toward a plan is to be settled (but not necessarily irrevocably) on executing it.[6] The intending and desiring attitudes toward plans differ in that the former alone entails this settledness. The distinctive practical nature of occurrent intentions to *A* distinguishes them from occurrent desires to *A*. A function of occurrent desires to *A*, as I understand them, is to help produce occurrent intentions to *A* (Mele 1992, chaps. 8 and 10); occurrent intentions are functionally more closely connected to intentional actions than are corresponding desires.

Most people recognize that intending to *A* differs from wanting or desiring to *A*. For example, you may occurrently want to eat a late snack (the cake is very tempting) while also occurrently wanting to refrain from eating it (you are concerned about your weight); but occurrently intending to eat a snack while occurrently intending to refrain from eating it (if this is possible) is a sign of a serious disorder. (Try to imagine that you intend to eat a snack now while also intending not to eat it now. What would you do? Would you reach for the snack with one hand and grab the reaching hand with your other hand?[7]) Similarly, this morning, you might want to meet a friend at noon for lunch, want to meet another friend at noon at a lecture, and be unsettled about what to do. At this point, you want to do each of these things and lack an intention about which of them to do. Making up your mind—that is, deciding—what to do would make sense. Again, as I understand deciding, to decide to *A* is to perform an action of forming an intention to *A* (Mele 2003, chap. 9).

Someone who desires to *A* (or to execute a certain plan for *A*-ing)—even someone who desires this more strongly than he desires not to *A* (or not to execute that plan)—may still be deliberating about whether to *A* (or about whether to execute the plan). In many such cases, at least, the agent is not settled on *A*-ing (or not settled on executing the plan).[8] Pat wants more strongly to respond in kind to a recent insult than to refrain from doing so, but owing to moral qualms, she is deliberating about whether to do so. She is unsettled about whether to retaliate despite the relative strength of her desires (see Mele 1992, chap. 9). Her unsettledness helps explain why she is deliberating about whether to retaliate.

On a standard view of desire, the psychological features of occurrent desires to $A$ in virtue of which they contribute to intentional $A$-ings are their content and their strength. On my view of the contribution of occurrent *intentions* to $A$ to intentional $A$-ings, the settledness feature of intentions is crucial, and it is not capturable in terms of desire strength (and content) nor in terms of this plus belief (Mele 1992, pp. 76–77 and chap. 9). Occurrent intentions to $A$, as I understand them, essentially encompass motivation to $A$ but without being reducible to a combination of desire and belief (Mele 1992, chap. 8). Part of what it is to be *settled* on $A$-ing is to have a motivation-encompassing attitude toward $A$-ing; lacking such an attitude, one lacks an element of a psychological commitment to $A$-ing that is intrinsic to being settled on $A$-ing and therefore to having an occurrent intention to $A$.

Many occurrent intentions come to be without being formed in acts of deciding. For example, "When I intentionally unlocked my office door this morning, I intended to unlock it. But since I am in the habit of unlocking my door in the morning and conditions...were normal, nothing called for a *decision* to unlock it" (Mele 1992, p. 231). If I had heard a fight in my office, I might have paused to consider whether to unlock the door or walk away, and I might have decided to unlock it. But given the routine nature of my conduct, there is no need to posit an action of intention formation in this case. My occurrent intention to unlock the door may have been acquired without having been actively formed. If, as I believe, all decisions about what to do are prompted partly by uncertainty about what to do (Mele 2003, chap. 9), in situations in which there is no such uncertainty, no decisions will be made. This is not to say that in such situations, no intentions will be acquired.

The sketch of a view of occurrent intentions that I have offered is background for much of this book. Readers interested in the details of a conceptual analysis of occurrent intentions or an account of their persistence may wish to consult Mele (2007). The sketch just offered suffices for present purposes. In the scientific work on intentions with which I am primarily concerned in this book, the focus is on occurrent intentions, not standing ones. Henceforth, when I use "intention" I mean "occurrent intention," unless I indicate otherwise.

I close this section with a comment on my action-variable *A* that is aimed at forestalling confusion. How readers interpret the variable should depend on their preferred theory of action individuation. Donald Davidson writes: "I flip the switch, turn on the light, and illuminate the room. Unbeknownst to me I also alert a prowler to the fact that I am home" (1980, p. 4). How many actions does the agent, Don, perform? Davidson's *coarse-grained* answer is one action "of which four descriptions have been given" (p. 4). A *fine-grained* alternative treats *A* and *B* as different actions if, in performing them, the agent exemplifies different act-properties (Goldman 1970). On this view, Don performs at least four actions because the act-properties at issue are distinct. An agent may exemplify any of these act-properties without exemplifying any of the others. (One may even turn on a light in a room without illuminating the room: the light may be painted black.) *Componential* views represent Don's illuminating the room as an action having various components, including his moving his arm (an action), his flipping the switch (an action), and the light going on (Ginet 1990). Where proponents of the coarse-grained and fine-grained theories find, respectively, a single action under different descriptions and a collection of intimately related actions, advocates of the various componential views locate a "larger" action having "smaller" actions among its parts. Readers should understand the variable *A* as a variable for actions themselves (construed componentially or otherwise) or actions under descriptions, depending on their preferred theory of action-individuation. The same goes for the expressions that take the place of *A* in concrete examples.

## 2. Proximal and Distal Intentions and Intentional Action

Some of our intentions are for the nonimmediate future, and others are not. I might have an intention on Thursday to pick up Angela at the airport on Saturday, and I might have an intention now to phone Nick now. The former intention is aimed at action two days in the future. The latter intention is about what to do now. I call intentions of these kinds, respectively, *distal* and *proximal* intentions (Mele 1992, pp. 143–44, 158). Proximal intentions also include intentions to continue doing something that one is doing and intentions to start *A*-ing (e.g., start running a mile) straightaway.

Some intentions have both proximal and distal aspects. For example, Al may have an intention to run a mile without stopping, beginning now. (He estimates that the deed will take six minutes.) I call such an intention a *mixed* intention. An intention of this kind specifies something to be done now and something to be done later. Just as there is no precise point of demarcation between men who count as bald and men who do not, there is no precise point of demarcation between intentions that count as proximal and intentions that count as mixed.

At least some intentions of all three kinds—distal, proximal, and mixed—are occurrent intentions. If my forming an intention on Thursday to pick up Angela at the airport on Sunday prompted me to make a note about that in my calendar, it was an occurrent intention at that time. Also, at any time at which I was conscious of that intention, it was an occurrent intention. If my acquiring a proximal intention to phone Nick issued straightaway in my dialing his number, that intention was an occurrent intention at that time. Similarly, if Al's acquiring the mixed intention I mentioned issued straightaway in his starting to run a mile, it was an occurrent intention at that time.

There are many competing philosophical views about the exact relation between items like intentions and brain states. A hypothesis that I explore in chapter 5 is intended to cohere with a wide variety of physicalistic views of this relation. It reads as follows:

> *H.* Whenever human beings perform an overt intentional action, at least one of the following plays a causal role in its production: some intention of theirs; the acquisition or persistence of some intention of theirs; the physical correlate of one or more of the preceding items.

Two terminological points are in order. First, the *physical correlate* relation, as I understand it, is *not* a causal relation.[9] There are other options, including the identity relation and various kinds of supervenience.[10] I am open minded (at least about this). Second, by *overt action,* I mean action that essentially involves peripheral bodily motion. Raising my hand essentially involves my hand rising, a peripheral bodily motion. When I calculate the gratuity on a dinner bill, I do it entirely in my head. In the United States, if nothing extraordinary has happened, I intentionally multiply the bill by 0.15. I do so independently of any peripheral bodily motion. My last calculation of a gratuity was *not* an overt action. Probably, the same will be true of my next one.

Some examples of relevant causal roles will prove useful. It may be that the acquisition of a proximal intention to answer a ringing phone (or the physical correlate of that event) directly or indirectly initiates motor commands that result in the agent's reaching toward the phone. The persistence of the intention (or the physical correlate of its persisting) may causally sustain the reaching. And the intention (or its physical correlate) may figure in the guidance of the motions of the arm and hand toward the phone. To save space, I often suppress parenthetical clauses about physical correlates; readers should supply them. Another space-saving measure I occasionally employ is to use "intentions (or their physical correlates)"—or simply "intentions"—as shorthand for the long disjunction in $H$.

There is considerable controversy in the philosophy of action about the exact meaning of "intentional" (and, accordingly, "intentionally"). Suppose that a novice darts player luckily succeeds in his first attempt to hit a bull's-eye. (He tries to repeat the feat another eighty times and fails.) Philosophers disagree about whether his hitting the bull's-eye counts as an intentional action.[11] But they agree that he intentionally threw the dart, intentionally threw it toward the dart board, and so on. Philosophers also disagree about what is done intentionally in scenarios featuring anticipated side effects (Bratman 1987; Harman 1976; Mele and Sverdlik 1996). Does a sniper who knows he will alert enemy soldiers to his presence when he fires at their leader but wishes he had a silencer on his rifle intentionally alert them to his presence? Or does he alert them knowingly but not intentionally? However these questions are answered, all parties can agree that the sniper does something intentionally: for example, he intentionally pulls the trigger. For proponents and opponents of $H$, what is important is that the player and the sniper performed *some* overt intentional action at the time. They can be noncommittal about whether the player's hitting the bull's-eye and the sniper's alerting the enemy are or are not intentional actions. (If the player's intention to throw the dart in the direction of the bull's-eye and the sniper's intention to fire at the enemy leader are among the causes of these intentional actions, they are also among the causes of the player's hitting the bull's-eye and the sniper's alerting the enemy whether or not the latter two actions count as intentional. In cases of these kinds, arguments for and against *H* can focus on actions that are uncontroversially intentional.)

I close this section with a motivational observation. The idea that intentions or their physical correlates play a causal role in the production of overt intentional actions is far from being a philosopher's pipe dream. As evidence for this assertion, I offer the following from the *Annual Review of Neuroscience*:

> We describe a potential medical application that utilizes the finding that the PPC [posterior parietal cortex] encodes movement intentions. The intention-related activity in the PPC can, in principle, be used to operate a neural prosthesis for paralyzed patients. Such a neural prosthesis would consist of recording the activity of PPC neurons, interpreting the movement intentions of the subject with computer algorithms, and using these predictions of the subject's intentions to operate external devices such as a robot limb or a computer. (Andersen and Buneo 2002, p. 190)

> The idea of a cortical prosthetic is to record...intentions to move, interpret the intentions using real-time decode algorithms running on computers, and then convert these decoded intentions to control signals that can operate external devices [including] stimulators imbedded in the patient's muscles that would allow the patient to move his/her own body, a robot limb, or a computer interface for communication. (Andersen and Buneo 2002, p. 213)

## 3. Decisions

Deciding to do something—practical deciding—must be distinguished from deciding that something is the case (for example, that a friend is likely to quit his job). In this section, I sketch an account of practical deciding defended in Mele

(2003, chap. 9). (Henceforth, I refer to practical decisions simply as decisions.)

As I mentioned in section 1, as I conceive of deciding to *A*, it is an action of forming an intention to *A*. On the conception that I favor, deciding is more specifically a *momentary* action of this kind (Mele 2003, chap. 9). Deliberating or reasoning about what to do definitely is not a momentary action, but it must be distinguished from an act of deciding that is based on deliberation. In my view, the momentary action of intention formation in which deciding to *A* consists is more fully an action of executive assent to a pertinent first-person plan of action (p. 210). In deciding to act, one forms an intention to act, and in so doing one brings it about that one has an intention that incorporates the plan to which one assents. The intention arises *in* the momentary intention-forming action, not after it.

My notion of executive assent is straightforward.[12] If you tell me that Mike is an excellent basketball player and I express complete agreement, I thereby assent to your claim. This is overt *cognitive* assent. If you propose that we watch Mike play tonight at the arena and I express complete acceptance of your proposal, I thereby assent to your proposal. This is overt *executive* assent. I have agreed to join you in executing your proposal for joint action. Now, perhaps my overt act of assenting to your proposal was a matter of giving voice to a nonactionally acquired intention to join you in watching Mike play. For example, on hearing your proposal, I might not have been at all uncertain about what to do; straightaway, I nonactionally acquired an intention to join you, and I voiced that intention in an overt act of assenting to your proposal. Or I might have weighed the pros and cons, judged that it would be best to join you, and, on the basis of that judgment, nonactionally acquired an intention to join you. However, there is also a distinctly different possibility. Perhaps, because I already had plans and because your offer was attractive, I was uncertain about what to do. Perhaps, on reflection, I judged that I could revise my plans without much inconvenience but was still uncertain about what to do, because my prior plans were attractive as well. And perhaps I performed a mental action of assenting to your proposal and then expressed that inner assent to you. In performing that mental action, if that is what occurred, I *decided* to join you: my mentally assenting to your proposal was an act of intention formation, an act of settling on joining you to watch Mike play tonight.

In Mele (2003), I reported on some of my common experiences of decision making (p. 202) and attempted to ascertain whether these experiences might be veridical. In the following three paragraphs, I reproduce my mundane examples.

Sometimes I find myself with an odd hour or less at the office between scheduled tasks or at the end of the day. Typically, I briefly reflect on what to do then. I find that I do not try to ascertain what it would be *best* to do at those times: this is fortunate, because settling that issue might take more time than it is worth. Rather, I look at a list of small tasks that need to be performed sooner or later—reply to an e-mail message, write a letter of recommendation, and the like—and decide which one to do. So, at least, it seems to me. Sometimes I have the experience not only of settling on a specific task or two but also, in the case of two or more tasks, of settling on a particular order of execution.

I have an e-mail system that plays a few musical notes when a message arrives. Occasionally, when I hear the notes, I pause briefly to consider whether to stop what I am doing and check the message. Sometimes I have the experience of deciding to check it or the experience of deciding not to check it. Sometimes I do not even consider checking the new message.

In situations of both of the kinds under consideration (the odd hour and incoming e-mail), I sometimes have the experience of having an urge to do one thing but deciding to do another instead. For example, when I hear that a new e-mail message has arrived, I may have an urge to check it straightaway but decide to finish what I am doing first. (When I am grading tests, these urges tend to be particularly strong.) When I am looking at my list of small tasks at the beginning of an odd hour, I may feel more inclined to perform one of the more pleasant tasks on my list but opt for a less pleasant one that is more pressing.

In this book, I leave it open whether all decisions are conscious decisions—that is, whether some momentary actions of executive assent to a first person plan of action are not consciously performed. If some of the experiences that I have just reported are not misleading, at least *some* decisions are conscious decisions. Attention to a recent argument that there are no conscious decisions may prove instructive.

Peter Carruthers seeks to defend Wegner's thesis that "conscious will is an illusion" (Carruthers 2007, p. 211). Carruthers contends that although some events of a certain kind "are conscious (such as mental rehearsal of the sentence 'I shall do Q'), and do play a causal role in the production of appropriate behavior, it isn't the right *sort* of causal role to constitute the event in question as an intention" (p. 212). He argues that conscious events cause actions only in a less direct way than the way in which proximal intentions and decisions are supposed to and that conscious intentions and decisions are therefore not part of the action-producing process. (In his view, their being part of this process requires their playing the relatively direct causal role they are supposed to play.) Carruthers writes: "only if I want to do what I have decided and *believe* that by saying to myself, 'I shall do Q' I *have* decided, does the action get settled upon" (p. 211). The "want" that he means to identify here is "a standing desire to do the things that I decide to do" (p. 208). He contends that "the inner verbalization isn't itself an intention to do Q, although it may play a causal role in the production of that action somewhat similar to that of an intention"

(p. 211). The alleged causal route here includes the desire and belief Carruthers specifies.

Carruthers believes that mental rehearsals of such sentences as "I shall do Q" are conscious. So, in principle, he should be willing to grant that in some cases, executive assent to a first-person plan of action is *conscious* executive assent. (On what grounds could one plausibly hold that although we sometimes consciously rehearse sentences, we never consciously engage in executive assent to a first-person plan of action?) Such assenting is an instance of consciously deciding to *A*, as I understand deciding. Now, some decisions are proximal decisions—momentary mental actions of proximal intention formation. On my view of proximal intentions, in ordinary circumstances, a direct effect of the intention's being formed or acquired (or of the physical correlate of that event) is the sending of appropriate motor signals (Adams and Mele 1992): the causal path from a proximal decision to *A*—conscious or otherwise—to a corresponding action definitely does not include the activation of a standing desire to do whatever one has decided nor a belief of the kind Carruthers identifies. Instead, in my view, the event of proximally deciding to *A* (or the physical correlate of that event) issues in a corresponding action in the relatively direct way Carruthers claims this is supposed to happen. Seemingly, Carruthers simply did not look hard enough for a conscious event that may plausibly be identified with, for example, my last proximal decision to check my e-mail and play the sort of role that proximal decisions are supposed to play. If he had looked harder, he would have found it difficult to claim that "only if I want to do what I have decided and *believe* that by saying to myself, 'I shall do Q' I *have* decided, does the action get settled upon" (2007, p. 211). Nothing recommends the judgment that actions can "get settled upon" only in this roundabout way, and that judgment plays a major role in Carruthers's argument that there are no conscious decisions.

Carruthers has failed to close the door on the possibility of conscious decisions. In chapter 2, I sketch a model of conscious deciding. In chapter 7, I review powerful evidence that conscious decisions play a role in the production of some corresponding intentional actions.

I argued for the existence of decisions as I conceive of them in Mele (2003, chap. 9). My strategy included cataloging ways in which intentions seemingly are nonactionally acquired—some of which have been mentioned here—and ascertaining what conceptual space might remain for momentary actions of intention formation. It also included a discussion of the phenomenology of decision making and an attempt to disarm what seem to be the main problems for the thesis that we make decisions. I have decided not to repeat the effort here. Interested readers will find chapter 9 of Mele (2003) a relatively easy read.

## 4. Preview

I close this chapter with a brief preview of this book. Chapter 2 is guided by two questions: Must proximal intentions be "conscious"? Why do scientists disagree about this? Chapters 3, 4, and 5 are critiques of some influential defenses by scientists of such bold claims as the following: your brain routinely decides what you will do before you become aware of its decision; there is only a 100-millisecond window of opportunity for free will; intentions and their physical correlates play no role in producing corresponding actions; and free will is an illusion. Chapter 6 examines the accuracy of subjects' reports about when they first became aware of proximal decisions or intentions in laboratory settings and develops some implications of warranted skepticism about the accuracy of these reports. Chapter 7 examines evidence of the effectiveness of conscious intentions and decisions of a certain kind. Chapter 8 wraps things up with a discussion of imaginary scientific findings that would warrant bold claims such as Libet's and Wegner's about free will, intentions, and decisions.

1. I defend this position in Mele (2003, chap. 9). Also see Frankfurt (1988, pp. 174–76), McCann (1986, pp. 254–55), Pink (1996, p. 3), and Searle (2001, p. 94).

2. Parts of the remainder of this section derive from Mele (2003, pp. 17, 27–28).

3. Roughly speaking, *basic* actions differ from nonbasic actions in not being performed by way of performing another action.

4. The guidance depends on the agent's monitoring progress toward his or her goal. The information (or misinformation) that Jan has entered her password, for example, figures in the etiology of her continued execution of her plan. On guidance, see Mele (2003, pp. 55–62).

5. Occurrent and standing desires may be distinguished from one another in a way that parallels the distinction I drew between occurrent and standing intentions. The same is true of occurrent and standing beliefs. See Mele (2007).

6. In the case of an intention for a not-doing (e.g., an intention not to vote tomorrow), the agent may instead be settled on not violating the simple plan embedded in it—the plan not to vote. On not-doings and attitudes toward them, see Mele 2003, pp. 146–54.

7. People who suffer from anarchic hand syndrome sometimes display behavior of this kind (Marchetti and Della Salla 1998). Sean Spence and Chris Frith suggest that these people "have conscious 'intentions to act' [that] are thwarted by ... 'intentions' to which the patient does not experience conscious access" (1999, p. 24).

8. A critic may claim that in all cases of this kind the agent is settled on a course of action without realizing it and

is deliberating only because he does not realize what he is settled on doing. For argumentation to the contrary, see Mele (1992, chap. 9).

9. I steer clear of the expression "neural correlate" because it is used in various distinct senses in the literature. "Physical correlate" is, I hope, a relatively innocuous technical term.

10. On supervenience, see Kim (2003).

11. Although Christopher Peacocke asserts that it is "undisputed" that an agent who makes a successful attempt "to hit a croquet ball through a distant hoop" intentionally hits the ball through the hoop (1985, p. 69), Brian O'Shaughnessy maintains that a novice who similarly succeeds in hitting the bull's-eye on a dart board does not intentionally hit the bull's-eye (1980, vol. 2, p. 325; also see Harman 1986, p. 92).

12. In the remainder of this paragraph, I borrow from Mele (2003, p. 210).

# TWO

# Conscious Intentions and Decisions

In chapter 1, I quoted Anthony Marcel's assertion that "Oddly, many psychologists seem to assume that intentions are by their nature conscious" (2003, p. 60). Daniel Wegner claims that "*Intention* is normally understood as an idea of what one is going to do that appears in consciousness just before one does it" (2002, p. 18). If this allegedly normal understanding of intention is treated as a *definition* of "intention," then, by definition, any item that does not "appear in consciousness" is not an intention, and intentions are "by their nature conscious." Is the connection between intentions and consciousness this tight? Why might scientists find themselves disagreeing about this? In sections 1 and 2, I lay some groundwork for an examination of these questions. In section 3, I offer some answers, to which I return in section 5. In section 4, I take up the related issue of the nature and possibility of conscious decisions. The conceptual and empirical background provided in this chapter facilitates the examination of the scientific work that is the subject matter of subsequent chapters.

The standard measure of subjects' consciousness of their intentions in scientific studies is reports subjects make to the effect that they were conscious of certain intentions at certain times. In the words of Richard Passingham and Hakwan Lau, "the operational index of consciousness is the ability to report" (2006, p. 67); notice that their assertion is about consciousness in general, whereas my assertion in the preceding sentence is just about consciousness of one's intentions. (I should add that one who does not realize that the operational index of the ability to report is an actual report may misread the quoted assertion.) Consciousness may be such that some occurrences or states that properly count as conscious for the ordinary adult human beings who are the loci of those occurrences or states are not reportable by those human beings. Unreportable consciousness is not my concern here. It is consciousness (or awareness) that is measurable by subjects' reports that concerns me; for it is consciousness of this kind, or in this sense, that is at issue in the dispute between Marcel and his opponents about whether "intentions are by their nature conscious." I call it *report-level consciousness* (or *awareness*). In the remainder of this chapter, I write simply in terms of consciousness (or awareness) and count on the reader to remember that report-level consciousness (or awareness) is at issue.

## 1. What Is the Question?

The view of occurrent intentions that I sketched in chapter 1 is based primarily on functions assigned to intention in various bodies of literature. If occurrent intentions are items of the kind described in chapter 1, must they be "conscious" for any of the following to play a significant role in producing intended actions: occurrent intentions, acquisitions of such intentions, the persistence of such intentions, or the physical correlates of any these things? As shorthand for what follows the colon in the preceding sentence, I often use the expression "intentions or their physical correlates."

A clearer formulation of the question just raised—question *Q*—would facilitate discussion. Obviously, if an intention is conscious, it is not conscious in the way in which I am conscious now. At the moment, I am conscious of the feel of my keyboard, the presence of my computer monitor, and a slight pain in my left elbow, among other things; and, of course, intentions are not conscious of anything. Is what is meant by a "conscious intention" of mine an intention of mine of which I am conscious? Wegner seems to mean something like this.[1] Recall his assertion that "*Intention* is normally understood as an idea of what one is going to do that appears in consciousness just before one does it" (2002, p. 18). He accepts this allegedly normal understanding and argues that intentions play no role in producing corresponding actions.

Wegner's account of intentions is unacceptable, as I explain shortly. My present concern is to get a grip on question Q. Here is one variant of it: (Q1) Must I be aware (or conscious) *of* my intention to A for it or its physical correlate to play a significant role in producing an intentional A-ing? Here is another: (Q2) Must I be aware (or conscious) *that* I intend to A for my intention to A or its physical correlate to play a significant role in producing an intentional A-ing? An agent's being aware that he intends to A entails that he has a concept of intention. Someone who has no concept of paradox or of counterfeit dollar bill—say, a normal two-year-old child—cannot be aware that his mother has just described a paradox to his sister or that he is holding a counterfeit bill. Similarly, someone who has no concept of intention—perhaps the same child—cannot be aware that he intends to A.[2] However, one can in principle be aware (or conscious) of an intention to A that one has without having a concept of intention and without being aware that one intends to A, just as one can be aware (or conscious) of a counterfeit bill without having a concept of counterfeit bill and without being aware, for example, that what one is looking at is a counterfeit bill. A young child who intends to pick up a toy that is lying on the floor a few feet away may, in principle, be conscious of something that we would describe as an intention to pick it up, even though he is in no position to describe—or conceive of—what he is conscious of in this way. Both *Q1* and *Q2* are targets of investigation here.

Return to Wegner's assertion that "*Intention* is normally understood as an idea of what one is going to do that appears in consciousness just before one does it" (2002, p. 18). This claim plainly does not apply to distal intentions (see chapter 1). Nor does it identify a sufficient condition for something being an intention. As you are driving, another driver cuts you off. The following idea of what you are "going to do . . . appears in consciousness just before" (Wegner, 2002) you hit his car: "Oh no! I'm going to hit that car." The idea expresses a prediction, not an intention; and "intention" definitely is not normally understood in such a way that this idea is an intention.

Perhaps what Wegner means is that proximal intentions, as normally understood, are ideas of what one is *intentionally* "going to do" that appear "in consciousness just before one does it" (in those cases in which one succeeds in doing what one proximally intends). Readers who do not *identify* proximal intentions with such ideas have some options about how to read Wegner's expression "conscious intention." For example, they may read it as referring to an intention that appears in consciousness *as an intention* or, instead, as referring to an intention some important aspect of which appears in consciousness. On the second reading, the aspect would apparently be some "idea of what one is going to do." Because the second reading is more modest, it is more charitable. One who thinks of occurrent intentions as executive attitudes toward plans (see chapter 1) may regard the content of the idea of what one is going to do that is supposed to appear in consciousness as including the content of a proximal intention or some important part or expression of the content.[3] (Again, in this view, the content of an intention is a plan.)

Might an agent have, at a time *t*, an occurrent intention to *A* without being conscious of it (or any part of it) at *t* and without being aware at *t* that he intends to *A*? In section 3, I argue that the answer is *yes.* I also argue there that this is the correct answer even on a very thin reading of "conscious intention" developed in the following section.

## 2. A Thin Reading of "Conscious Intention"

Might one underestimate the frequency of "conscious" proximal intentions as a consequence of framing one's search for them in terms of such things as agents' awareness that they *intend* to *A* or their awareness of (some aspect of) their proximal *intentions* to *A*? Might it be useful to think in terms of agents' awareness (or consciousness) of being *about to A*, where that is not a predictive awareness of the sort present in the case of the driver who is aware that he is about to collide with the car that just cut him off?

Consider an artificial scenario. As I was sitting at my desk thinking about conscious intentions, I decided to raise my right arm later and pay very close attention to what I am aware of and how things feel just before I begin to raise it. My plan was to count slowly and silently and begin raising my arm when I got to five. Some time later, I did this. I was aware that I was about to raise my right arm. Seemingly, that awareness was based at least partly on my awareness that I intended to raise my arm when I got to five and my awareness that I was approaching five.

Wegner speaks of an "authorship emotion"—a "feeling of doing" (2002, p. 325). If there is such a feeling, there may also be an anticipatory feeling of being about to perform an action of a specific kind. (Set yourself the task of slowly raising your right arm when you have slowly and silently counted to five and paying very close attention to what you are aware of and how things feel just before you begin to raise it. Did you notice something that might reasonably be described as a *feeling* of being about to raise your arm?)

Consider a scenario that is not at all artificial. Normally, when I get home from work, I park my car in the driveway, walk to my side door, unlock it, open it, and walk into the kitchen, closing the door behind me. It is natural to say that all of these actions are intentional and intended. Normally, I am aware (conscious) of doing them and of my driveway, my door, and my keys. Is it also true that normally, when I am about to unlock my door, I am aware that I am about to unlock it? Attention to some contrasting scenarios might help in articulating what this kind of awareness might be like.

Consider a scenario in which things proceed routinely until I try to turn my key in the lock. This time, the key does not move, and the door, consequently, is not unlocked. The lock is jammed. Now, "S is about to unlock his door" does not entail "S proceeds to unlock his door," as the following true story indicates: "Ann was about to unlock her door when she heard someone call her from the street. She immediately walked toward the street, keys in hand, to see who was calling." It is true that Ann was about to unlock her door even though she did not unlock it, and the same may be true of me in the jammed lock scenario. This provides some guidance for someone seeking to understand what it means to say that I am aware that I am about to unlock my door. I return to this suggestion after presenting another contrasting scenario.

As I am walking on a crowded sidewalk, the person in front of me suddenly stops. I am aware that I am about to bump into him even as I try to minimize the collision. My awareness here is based on observation of external events and my sense of how fast I am moving and how quickly I can stop. On this basis, I *predict* the bump. My awareness that I am about to bump into the person in front of me is an instance of what may be called *predictive awareness*. My awareness that I am about to sneeze also is a predictive awareness, even though that awareness normally is not even partly based on my observation of external events.

When, in a normal scenario, I am aware that I am about to unlock my door, on what is that awareness based? One may claim that it is based solely on nonintrospective observation: I see that I am approaching the door and I feel or see the keys in my hand; I infer from this that I am about to unlock my door. Is this plausible? Seemingly not; and on a thin reading of "conscious intention," the following is sufficient for my having a *conscious* proximal intention to unlock my door: my having a proximal intention to unlock my door together with an awareness that I am about to unlock it that differs from what I called *predictive awareness*. Naming the kind of awareness that I have just contrasted with predictive awareness promotes economy of expression. I name it *type 1 awareness*, and I call predictive awareness *type 2 awareness*. If type 1 awareness is a real phenomenon, it has at least a partial basis in something other than nonintrospective observation. Possibly, if Wegner were to offer a position on the content of ideas of what one is going to do that he identifies with intentions, he would understand that content as the content of states of type 1 awareness. Partly because I have not offered an *account* of type 1 awareness, the proposed sufficient condition of my having a conscious proximal intention to unlock my door definitely is open to interpretation. I wish to leave reasonable but relatively undemanding interpretations of the condition open because I want to show that even when the standards for a proximal intention's being a conscious intention are relatively modest, it is implausible that all proximal intentions are conscious. (Here, a reminder that the consciousness or awareness at issue are at the *report level* may be in order.)

A disjunctive alleged sufficient condition of an agent's having a conscious proximal intention to *A* may be constructed out of the various sufficient conditions for this suggested in this section: the agent's being aware of his proximal intention to *A* or of some appropriate part or expression of its content; the agent's being aware that he intends to *A* now;

the agent's having a proximal intention to *A* together with a type 1 awareness that he is about to *A*. Another disjunct may be added to the list: a proximal intention to *A* may be treated as a conscious proximal intention at a time if, at that time, the agent consciously makes a proximal *decision* to *A*. (On conscious deciding, see section 4.)

## 3. Questions Answered: Functional Roles and Folk Theories

Why might researchers disagree about whether all proximal intentions are conscious intentions, even on the broad disjunctive reading of conscious proximal intention that I sketched? One possible explanation is that even setting aside the issue of consciousness, they disagree about what intentions are. A potential source of this dispute is disagreement about what does and does not count as an intentional action. Disagreement about the latter issue is a convenient place to start in pursuing this section's focal question.

If some theorists have a more restrictive conception of intentional action than others do, it might not be surprising that they also have a more restrictive conception of intention. In chapter 1, I described my view that occurrent intentions are executive attitudes toward plans. My route to that view (in Mele 1992, chap. 8) starts with canvassing functions attributed to intentions—or, more precisely, to intentions, their acquisition, their persistence, or physical correlates of these things. (Reminder: I often use the expression "intentions or their physical correlates" as shorthand for this.) The featured functions include (but are not limited to) initiating, sustaining, and guiding intentional actions. Someone who agrees that intentions or their physical correlates play these roles but disagrees with me about what counts as an intentional action may also disagree with me, accordingly, about what intentions are. That disagreement may have a bearing on our respective views about the connection between intentions and consciousness.

The following assertion from an article by neuroscientists Patrick Haggard and Sam Clark is interesting in this connection: "functional imaging studies of intentional actions typically show activation in the basal ganglia and supplementary motor area...while studies of externally triggered actions show activation in the cerebellum and premotor cortex" (2003, pp. 695–96). This assertion certainly suggests that "externally triggered actions" are not intentional actions. One study Haggard and Clark cite compares subjects instructed to raise their right index fingers whenever they wish without waiting more than four seconds between raisings with subjects instructed to raise their right index fingers whenever they hear a tone (Jahanshahi et al. 1995). (The tones are separated by no more than four seconds.) The first group are said to perform "self-initiated" finger raisings and the second to perform "externally triggered" finger raisings (Jahanshahi et al. 1995, p. 913). As I use "intentional," the finger raisings of both groups are obviously intentional. As Haggard and Clark use "intentional," the finger raisings of the second group are not intentional.

How might this difference in usage bear on a disagreement about the connection between consciousness and intention? Marjan Jahanshahi and coauthors infer that the greater activation of the dorsolateral prefrontal cortex in the first group "was associated with the additional requirement of *decision making* about the timing of the movement on each trial, or 'when to do' it" (1995, p. 930; emphasis added); this is what motivates Haggard and Clark's claim about which finger raisings are intentional and which are not.[4] Haggard and Clark surely would find it odd to say that although the finger raisers in the second group do not intentionally raise their index fingers, they *intend* to raise them. So they probably equate intentions with decisions or think that the only way we acquire intentions to *A* is by deciding to *A*.

If this is their view, then if my claim in chapter 1 that not all intentions are acquired in acts of decision making is correct, Haggard and Clark have an unduly restrictive conception of intention—to which their restrictive conception of intentional action might have led them. Notice finally that if it is significantly more plausible that agents consciously make all of their decisions than that agents consciously acquire all of their intentions (including intentions not acquired in acts of decision making), theorists with a view of intentional action like Haggard and Clark's are more likely, other things equal, to view intentions as being essentially conscious than are theorists with a broader—and, I daresay, more normal—conception of intentional action. (Recall that by "decisions," I mean *practical* decisions—decisions about what to *do*.) One moral is that one who wishes to appeal to empirical assertions about intentions should try to get a firm sense of what the researchers making the assertions mean by "intention."

The standard measure of awareness of intentions in scientific studies, as I have mentioned, is subjects' reports. For example, Benjamin Libet (1985) asked his subjects to report, after flexing a wrist, on when they first became aware of a proximal intention to flex it (or some related state, see following discussion). The subjects, instructed to flex whenever they felt like it, were watching a rapidly revolving dot on a clock and trying to keep track of where the dot was when they first became aware of a proximal intention to flex (or some related state).

Suppose experienced drivers in the habit of signaling for the turns they make were asked to drive for an hour in an area used for teaching novice drivers; to turn at whatever intersections they felt like turning at, using their indicators to signal the turns; and to report after flipping the indicator on when they first became aware of their intention to flip it. They are instructed to keep track of a rapidly revolving dot on a clock on their rearview mirrors as they drive and make their awareness reports in terms of where the dot was when they first became aware of the pertinent intentions. Such a study might generate many reports of intention awareness. The instructions would encourage subjects to search their minds, as it were, for intentions to flip their turn indicators. If they do become aware of proximal intentions to flip them, one hypothesis is that what they become aware of are states of a kind—proximal intentions—that would have been present under normal circumstances without their being aware of them. In experienced drivers who are in the habit of signaling for their turns, the signaling is "overlearned" or "automatic" behavior: in normal circumstances, they often are not aware of doing it, much less of being about to do it or of having a proximal intention to do it.[5]

The hypothesis I just mentioned is of special interest in connection with the central thesis of Wegner's *Illusion of Conscious Will* (2002). Wegner argues that "conscious will is an illusion . . . in the sense that *the experience of consciously willing an action is not a direct indication that the conscious thought has caused the action*" (2002, p. 2). He contends that "the experience of will is merely a feeling that occurs to a person" (p. 14). More specifically, "conscious will . . . is a feeling of doing" (p. 325). He writes: "The new idea introduced here is the possibility that the experience of acting develops when the person infers that his or her own *thought* (read intention, but belief and desire are also important) was the cause of the action" (p. 66). Collectively, these last three quotations suggest that his claim about illusion may be understood as follows: the feeling of doing "an action is not a direct indication that the conscious [intention to perform the action] has caused the action."

Among the work to which Wegner appeals his thesis about illusion is that of Libet. In experiment, subjects are instructed to flex thei or the fingers of their right hands whenever they Electrical readings from the scalp (EEGs)—ave least forty flexings for each subject—show a shift in "readiness potentials" (RPs) beginning about 550 ms before the time at which an electromyogram (EMG) shows relevant muscular motion to begin. Subjects are also instructed to "recall...the spatial clock position of a revolving spot at the time of [their] initial awareness" (p. 529) of something, $x$, that Libet variously describes as an "intention," "urge," "wanting," "decision," "will," or "wish" to flex.[6] On average, RP onset preceded what the subjects reported to be the time of their initial awareness of $x$ (time W) by 350 ms. Reported time W, then, preceded the beginning of muscle motion by about 200 ms. These results may be represented as follows.

TABLE 2.1. Libet's Results

| −550 ms | −200 ms | 0 ms |
|---|---|---|
| RP onset | reported time W | muscle begins to move |

(Libet finds independent evidence of what he regards as an error in subjects' recall of the times at which they first become aware of sensations. Correcting for it, time W is −150 ms.[7])

Wegner writes: "The position of conscious will in the time line suggests perhaps that the experience of will is a link in a causal chain leading to action, but in fact it might not even be that. It might just be a loose end—one of those things, like the action, that is caused by prior brain and mental events" (2002, p. 55). By "the experience of will" in this passage, Wegner means "the experience of wanting to move" (p. 55). He is suggesting that this is not a cause of the flexing. Here one must be careful (see Bayne 2006; Hardcastle 2004; Holton 2004). A subject's wanting to flex soon and his experience of wanting to flex soon are not the same thing. So to grant that a subject's experience of wanting to flex soon is not a cause of his flexing is not to grant that his wanting to flex soon also is not a cause of his flexing. My flipping a light switch—not my *experience* of flipping it—is a cause of the light going on. Analogously, a subject's wanting to flex soon may be a cause of his flexing even if his experience of wanting to flex soon is not.[8]

Move from wanting to intending. An intention to flex straightaway is a proximal intention. Suppose that Libet's subjects have many conscious intentions of this kind during the course of an experiment. Suppose also that neither their *experiences* of proximally intending to flex nor the physical correlates of those experiences are causes of their flexing actions. These suppositions leave it open that the subjects' proximal intentions or their physical correlates are causes of these actions; for their experiences of their proximal intentions are not identical with the intentions themselves.

Partly because they are told that they need to "recall ... the spatial clock position of a revolving spot at the time of [their] initial awareness" of their urges (or wishes, intentions, etc.) to flex (Libet 1985, p. 529), some of Libet's subjects may interpret their instructions as including an instruction to wait until they *feel*—that is, experience—an urge to flex before they flex and to flex in response to that feeling. If they comply with the instructions, so understood, the feelings are among the causes of the flexings: the feelings serve as cues to begin flexing. This obvious point is a problem for Wegner's *statement* of his position—specifically, his claim that "the experience of wanting to move" in Libet's subjects is not "a link in a causal chain leading to action" (2002, p. 55). However, Wegner's actual position is more subtle. It is that the basic causal process that leads to flexing in these subjects does not depend on consciousness of (that is, feeling) an urge to flex. The idea is that even if the subjects were not waiting to feel an urge as a cue for flexing—even if, as one might put it, they did not interpret an instruction to flex whenever they *feel* like it in a phenomenological way—flexing would be produced in the same basic way: their consciousness of the urge is "just ... a loose end" in this process (Wegner 2002, p. 55), and the same is true of their consciousness of any proximal intention to flex that may emerge.

Suppose that Wegner is right about this. What would the upshot be? If, as Marcel (2003) maintains, nonconscious proximal intentions can produce corresponding intentional actions, an agent's conscious proximal intention to flex may produce a flexing action in a way that does not depend on it being a *conscious* intention. If many proximal intentions produce actions without the intentions showing up in consciousness, this is not a terribly surprising result.

In an imaginary variant of Libet's main experiment in which subjects are asked to watch the clock and flex whenever they feel like it but are not asked to report on their awareness of anything, would consciousness of a mental antecedent of flexing be a frequent occurrence? A bit of personal background helps set the stage for discussion.

I was once a subject in an experiment with the design of Libet's main experiment. I had just three things to do: watch the clock with a view to keeping track of when I first became aware of something in the ballpark of a proximal urge or intention to flex; flex whenever I felt like it (many times); and report, after each flex, where I believed the dot was on the clock at the moment of first awareness. (I reported this belief by moving a cursor to a point on the clock.) Because I found it difficult to locate a specific proximal urge or intention or a feeling of being about to flex, I hit on the strategy of saying "now!" silently to myself just before beginning to flex. This is the mental event that I tried to keep track of with the assistance of the clock. I thought of the "now!" as shorthand for the imperative "flex now!"—something that may be understood as an expression of a proximal decision to flex. (To make a proximal decision to flex is to form—actively—a proximal intention to flex.)

Suppose that my task had been simply to flex whenever I felt like it (many times) while watching the clock. One might think that because the only salient practical question facing me during the experiment would be when to flex, I would be aware of some distinctive kind of occurrence that preceded the flexings. The thought, perhaps, is that I would be aware of a distinctive antecedent of the flexings because there is so little to attend to in this experiment. However, when I try this, I find that I am not aware of such an antecedent. Nor am I alone in this: see Bruno Breitmeyer's remarks on his own experience and that of several colleagues (1985, p. 539). I needed the silent "now!" in the actual experiment to have some mental event that I could report, but I do not need it in the modified experiment. (If I were to hit on the strategy of silently saying "now!" to myself to answer my practical question about when to flex in the imagined experiment, how would I answer my practical question about when to say "now!"?)

Suppose that in the imagined experiment, I were to display RPs of just the sort I displayed in the actual experiment. A proponent of Wegner's view may contend that the supposed result would indicate that proximal intentions to flex (and their physical correlates) are not involved in the production of my flexings in either experiment, even if I have a "conscious" proximal intention to flex in the actual experiment. One argument for this contention runs as follows. (1) The RPs are correlated with the causes of the flexing; (2) that the RPs match each other indicates that the causes at work in the two experiments are of the same kind; (3) given that intentions are essentially conscious, there is no proximal intention to flex in the imaginary experiment; and, obviously, absent intentions can do no causal work; so (4) given that the causes at work in the two experiments are of the same kind, my proximal intention to flex does no causal work in the actual experiment.

The argument is unconvincing, even if its first two premises are granted. The supposed result is consistent with the view that proximal intentions to flex (or their physical correlates) are at work in me in both experiments, provided that proximal intentions are not essentially conscious.[9] Libet's experimental design may foster consciousness of proximal intentions to flex, and those intentions (or their physical correlates) may do their action-initiating work independently of the subjects' consciousness of them. They may do the same work when agents are not conscious of them.

In my own case, as I mentioned, Libet's experimental design seemingly prompted me, in effect, to make conscious decisions about when to flex so that I would have a mental event to report. If to decide to A is to perform the momentary action of forming an intention to A (see chapter 1), then in proximally deciding to flex, I formed a proximal intention to flex. Insofar as I consciously made my proximal decisions to flex, the associated proximal intentions may be counted as conscious intentions. But in principle, proximal intentions to flex that are acquired without being formed in acts of proximal deciding may do the same basic work as these conscious intentions.

Compare my unlocking my side door with a normal experienced driver's flipping the turn indicator for a turn he is about to make in utterly normal circumstances. When, in normal circumstances, I unlock my door and walk into my kitchen after driving home from work, the claim that I am aware of unlocking the door and walking into the kitchen certainly is significantly less controversial than the claim that I was aware of being about to do these things. Because experienced drivers seem typically not to be aware of flipping their turn signals in normal circumstances, the claim that they are aware of being about to flip them rests on shaky ground. However, this places the claim that they have proximal intentions to flip them on similarly shaky ground only on the assumption that proximal intentions are essentially conscious, even on the modest disjunctive understanding of "conscious proximal intention" that I identified. And that conceptual assumption is far from unassailable.

In an article defending the thesis that "most of a person's everyday life is determined not by their conscious intentions and deliberate choices but by mental processes that are put into motion by features of the environment and that operate outside of conscious awareness and guidance" (1999, p. 462), John Bargh and Tanya Chartrand approvingly quote (p. 468) the following passage from William James's *The Principles of Psychology*: "It is a general principle in Psychology that consciousness deserts all processes where it can no longer be of use.... We grow unconscious of every feeling which is useless as a sign to lead us to our ends, and where one sign will suffice others drop out, and that one remains, to work alone" (1890, vol. 2, p. 496). If James is right, by the time drivers have developed the habit of signaling for turns they are about to make, they no longer consciously form intentions to signal for turns (in normal circumstances) and no longer are conscious of being about to signal or even of signaling (in normal circumstances). Even so, in a straightforward sense of "intentional," their signalings are intentional actions; in light of this, it certainly is far from bizarre to suggest that they are intended.[10] Bargh and Chartrand write, "goals can become activated by means other than an act of will, and once activated, such goals operate in the same way, and produce the same effects, as when they are put into motion intentionally" (p. 472). Similarly, a conscious and a nonconscious proximal intention to signal for a turn may "operate" in basically the same way and produce a signaling action. One who takes the position that all proximal intentions are conscious intentions produced by conscious acts of will, as Bargh and Chartrand seem to do, will reject the preceding sentence. But what motivates this position seems to be its adherents' sensitivity to what they take to be a popular folk theory about intentions or the folk concept of intention, not empirical considerations. To the extent to which proximal intentions are conceptualized in terms of such roles as initiating, sustaining, and guiding intentional actions, such actions being understood as including normal experienced drivers' signaling for turns in normal circumstances, the postulation of nonconscious proximal intentions is attractive.

I opened this chapter with Marcel's assertion that "oddly, many psychologists seem to assume that intentions are by their nature conscious (2003, p. 60). He produces what he regards as counterexamples, including the following:

> The expert acts intentionally but may be unaware of the specifics of tactical intentions, for example, in tennis whether one intends to play a drop volley or a drive volley even when the postural aspects of one's approach to the net is a selective preparation for one rather than the other. Indeed, this is why even when such experts sincerely claim unawareness of their intention, their opponent can anticipate the shot, though the opponent himself may not know how he did so. (Marcel, 2003, p. 61)

Marcel does not say here whether, when the player begins his stroke, he is still unaware of his intention to hit whatever sort of shot he intends to hit—a drive volley, say. But he is at least claiming, in effect, that as the player is running to the net, he has a proximal (or mixed) intention to put himself in a position to hit a drive volley without being aware of that. As I understand Marcel, the player does not have a conscious intention to do this in any of the senses of "conscious intention" that I identified. When the player starts moving toward the net, he is not aware of being about to begin putting himself in a position to hit a drive volley; and as he is moving toward the net, he is not aware that he is putting himself in a position to hit such a volley.

Why does this seem right to Marcel? Because, unlike Wegner, Bargh and Chartrand, and others, he conceives of proximal intentions in terms of such functional roles as initiating, sustaining, and guiding intentional actions, and he does not take an agent's intentionally $A$-ing to require being conscious (aware) of $A$-ing. It is not at all odd that scientists who conceive of intentions in this way would reject the assumption that intentions are by their nature conscious. Nor is it odd that they would find their opponents' view odd.

Can an agent *A* intentionally without being aware of *A*-ing? If a driver can intentionally flip his turn signal without being aware of flipping it and a tennis pro can intentionally put himself in a position to hit a drive volley without being aware that he is putting himself in a position to do that, then the answer is *yes*. These examples are controversial in the present context, but others are not. Consider the following case (Mele 2001a, p. 36). Al knows that funny jokes about cows have consistently made his young daughter laugh. When he composes and sends a funny e-mail message about cows to his daughter with the intention of making her laugh, he is not aware that she is laughing and therefore is not aware that he is making her laugh. Suppose that when she reads the joke, she finds it hilarious and laughs uproariously. Then it is very plausible that Al *intentionally* makes her laugh, given the other details of the case. To be sure, Al was aware of doing some of the things that he did intentionally in this story: for example, he was aware of composing a message about cows. But making his daughter laugh is not among the things he was aware of doing. One who claims that intentionally *A*-ing entails being aware of *A*-ing is considering too narrow a range of examples of intentional action.

Some neuroscientists are doing research with monkeys aimed at developing neural prostheses that will enable paralyzed people to move their limbs. They seek to record monkeys' intentions and use the associated neural signals to move robot arms, for example (see Andersen and Buneo 2002, quoted in chapter 1; Musallam, Corneil, Greger, Scherberger, and Andersen 2004). Recall that the standard measure of awareness of intentions in scientific studies is subjects' reports. The monkeys in these experiments report nothing. Yet in the articles I cited, the experimenters express no reservations about attributing intentions to them. Presumably, if they had shared Wegner's conception of intentions as essentially conscious, they would have sought evidence of the required consciousness.

I return to this section's central topics in my concluding section. The next item of business harks back to the preceding section.

## 4. Conscious Decisions

I closed section 2 with the assertion that a proximal intention to A may be treated as a *conscious* proximal intention at a time if, at that time, the agent consciously makes a proximal decision to A. In chapter 1, I sketched an account of practical deciding—deciding to *do* something. But what does *consciously* deciding to A amount to? Is such deciding even possible? These questions guide this section. Because attention to them will prove useful in subsequent chapters, I pursue them in greater depth here than would be called for if my aim were simply to provide information about one of the disjuncts in my disjunctive sufficient condition for a proximal intention being a conscious intention. My approach to motivating some answers is indirect. It features attention to my silent "now!" sayings as a subject in a Libet-style experiment.

Consider the following thesis: (T) The onset of awareness or consciousness of any event has the onset of the event among its causes and there is no simultaneous causation. For example, if the onset of my awareness of a light flashing has the onset of the light flashing among its causes and there is no simultaneous causation, then the onset of the light flashing precedes the onset of my awareness of its flashing. Is thesis T true? If it is, then, for example, the onset of my silently saying "now!" to myself as a subject in a Libet-style experiment precedes the onset of my awareness or consciousness of that silent speech act. Is that how it (always) is? Can it ever happen that I silently say "now!" and the onset of my awareness or consciousness of performing that silent action is simultaneous with the onset of the action? Can I consciously perform the silent action, in a sense of "consciously perform" that requires my being conscious of performing the action the whole (very brief) time I am performing it?

If the correct model for consciously performing the silent speech act is becoming conscious of an external event—for example, a light flashing—then the correct answer to the last question I asked is *no*. In the case of becoming conscious of an external event, that event—or at least its onset—occurs before we are conscious of the event and before we are conscious of any segment of the event. There is a causal connection between the event's onset, on one hand, and our becoming conscious of the event and of any segment of the event, on the other; and causation (in this sphere, at least) takes time. But is this the correct model?

Before I answer this question, an issue about event segments requires attention. Consider an analogy. As Ann is strolling through a zoo, she notices the elephant house, and she eagerly heads toward it. She soon catches sight of an elephant's trunk and head. Does she see the elephant? Saying *yes* is not misleading, even though she has not yet seen the whole elephant. Similarly, it is not misleading to say that I can become conscious of an event at a time at which the whole event has not yet occurred—that I can become conscious of an event while it is in progress. If we choose to speak this way, we should not say that consciousness of external events arises only after the events have *occurred*. We should say instead that consciousness of external events arises only after the events have *begun*. If we speak this way, we also should be careful not to confuse the beginning of an event with a cause of the event. The beginning of an event is an early segment of the event. The time of the *onset* of *x*, for any $x$, is the time of $x$'s initial presence or of the occurrence of its earliest segment.

I return to my question about consciously performing a silent speech act of saying "now!" to myself. Is the correct model for this becoming conscious of an external event? Consider the Frölich effect: "a slit of light moving at a constant speed from the left edge (say) into a window on a screen is first seen at some distance from the left edge, never at the left edge" (van de Grind 2002, p. 252). Why? Because, as Wim van de Grind puts it, it takes time for the visual system to determine "a position signal for a moving target and the calculation involves averaging a range of previous positions, so that it never gives you the starting position" (2002, p. 252). Processing input from the external world takes time; so vision lags behind the occurrence of events or event segments that one sees. (In the case of the moving slit of light, it is not as though one does not see the slit move until it has completed its movement into the window, that is, until that event is over; however, one does not begin to see the slit at all until it has already moved some distance, and one's vision of it lags behind its progress across the screen.) Now any occurrence of my silently saying "now!" as a subject in a Libet-style experiment is undoubtedly the result of a causal process. That process—like any process—takes time. What that process might issue in is my consciously performing the speech act at issue in the sense of "consciously perform" that I identified in this section—one that requires my being conscious of performing the action the whole (very brief) time I am performing it. There is no sound conceptual argument for the assertion that I become conscious of my silent speech act only after the action itself—*as opposed to a process that gives rise to it*—is under way. And there is no sound empirical argument for this. Consciousness of the speech act need not lag behind (segments of) the act in the way that vision of external events lags behind (segments of) the events seen.

Have I suddenly become a substance dualist?[11] Not at all. A proper causal, physical account of the production of my conscious silent speech act can diverge from a proper causal, physical account of the onset of consciousness of external events. In the latter case, the external events are among the causes of consciousness of them and we become conscious of events that have already begun or already happened. But my consciously saying "now!" to myself need not be a matter of my becoming conscious of a "now!" saying that has already begun. Again, the causal process at work may instead issue in a speech act that is a conscious act right from its onset. And again, the onset of an action should not be confused with anything that precedes the action.

The view of conscious, silent "now!" saying that I have sketched provides a model for understanding an agent's consciously deciding to *A* or at least some instances of such deciding. Recall that in my view, to decide to *A* is to perform a momentary action of forming an intention to *A*. Deciding to *A*, as I conceive of it, is not to be confused with any process that issues in a decision to *A*, including, for example, deliberation about what to do. And deciding to *A* does not precede the onset of the intention to *A* formed in the act of deciding. Instead, what it is to decide to *A* is to form—actively—an intention to *A*. The intention arises *in* that momentary intention-forming action, not after it.

I have suggested that I can consciously perform a silent "now!" saying action in a sense of "consciously perform" that requires my being conscious of performing the action the whole (very brief) time I am performing it. I now suggest that I can consciously decide to *A*—that is, consciously perform the momentary action of forming an intention to *A*—in the same sense of "consciously perform." (Just as my parallel suggestion about conscious "now!" saying is utterly compatible with a nondualistic view of action production, so is this suggestion about conscious deciding.) If the latter suggestion is correct, the time of the onset of a proximal intention to *A* can—at least sometimes—be identical with the time of the onset of the agent's consciousness or awareness of that intention. These times are identical whenever an agent consciously decides to *A* in the sense of "consciously decide" just sketched—a sense requiring that the agent be conscious of the deciding-to-*A* action the whole (very brief) time he is performing it.

## 5. Conclusion

In the opening paragraph of this chapter, I raised two questions: Are intentions by their nature conscious? Why might scientists find themselves disagreeing about this? In the scientific literature on intentions discussed in this chapter, the focus is *proximal* intentions. Accordingly, I narrowed the focus of the first question to intentions of this kind. I identified various interpretations of "conscious intention," including a very modest one according to which the following is sufficient for having a conscious proximal intention to *A*: having a proximal intention to *A* together with an awareness that one is about to *A* that differs from what I called predictive awareness. And I motivated the thesis that given any of the interpretations offered, not all proximal intentions are conscious intentions.

My answer to the second question, in a nutshell, is this: some scientists conceive of proximal intentions in terms of such functional roles as initiating, sustaining, and guiding intentional actions and they do not take an agent's intentionally *A*-ing to require that he is conscious (aware) of *A*-ing, whereas others conceive of proximal intentions in a way that is motivated by their sensitivity to an apparent folk theory about or folk concept of such intentions according to which they are all conscious products of conscious acts of will. Obviously, scientists are free to use the word "intention" as they see fit, but they should make their meanings clear. Lack of clarity can result not only in misunderstanding or puzzlement on the part of readers but also in misunderstanding the import of one's own data.

Whether layfolk conceive of proximal intentions as uniformly conscious products of conscious acts of will is testable. For example, researchers can ask one group of experienced drivers whether, when they signal for turns, they intend to do that; and they can ask other groups of equally experienced drivers such questions as whether, in normal circumstances, they are aware of an intention to signal for a turn they are about to make, aware that they intend to signal, and aware of being about to signal. If it were to turn out that *yes* is the majority response to the first question and *no* is the majority response to each of the questions about awareness, that would be evidence that the folk concept of proximal intention does not treat proximal intentions as essentially conscious. But this imagined discovery about a folk concept—a discovery that would imply, for example, that Wegner overestimated the extent to which layfolk link intentions to consciousness—is not a discovery about how actions are produced. If, as James says, "consciousness deserts all processes where it can no longer be of use" (1890, vol. 2, p. 496), and if many such processes survive the desertion, then perhaps it deserts some processes that include proximal intentions and corresponding intentional actions while those intention-including processes survive. Whether this is so does not depend on whether layfolk (or some researchers) happen to conceive of proximal intentions as essentially conscious.

My reason for focusing on *proximal* intentions is that they are the focus of most of the scientific work on intentions discussed in this book. Consider the claim that all effective occurrent *distal* intentions are, at some time or other, conscious intentions. There is more to recommend this claim than there is to recommend the corresponding claim about effective proximal intentions.[12] Setting fanciful hypotheses aside, if distal intentions of mine to write a grant proposal next month, to send my sister a birthday card next week, or to buy a plane ticket to Berlin after I return home from Idaho were never conscious intentions, I would not act on them (in which case they would not be what I call *effective* intentions). Possibly, those who say that intentions are essentially conscious take effective occurrent distal intentions as their model of what intentions are, judge that all such intentions are (at some time or other) conscious intentions, and (tacitly) assume that regarding consciousness, what is true of effective occurrent distal intentions is true of all occurrent intentions. However, empirical work focused on *proximal* intentions is well served by conceptual work on the same topic.

In the introduction to this chapter, I reported that conceptual and empirical background provided here facilitates my examination of scientific work in subsequent chapters. Readers will not have to trust me about this for long.

NOTES

1. For two occurrences of "conscious intention," see Wegner (2002, pp. 20 and 68).

2. Janet Astington and Alison Gopnik suggest that "at four or five years of age children begin to differentiate intention from desire" (1991, p. 47).

3. See Elisabeth Pacherie's distinction between what she calls first- and second-order consciousness and her application of it to the interpretation of "conscious intention" (2006, pp. 160, 164).

4. Notice that as I understand deciding and intention acquisition (see chapter 1), we apparently have physical evidence of a difference between proximally deciding to $A$ and otherwise acquiring a proximal intention to $A$ (but for a

relevant caveat, see Jahanshahi et al. 1995, p. 930). For evidence that activity in the presupplementary motor area is associated specifically with deciding, see Lau, Rogers, Ramnani, and Passingham (2004).

5. If the turn indicator were to become stuck, these drivers probably would notice that. But that does not entail that they were aware of (some aspect of) their intention to flip it or of being about to flip it or that they were aware that they intended to flip it. Awareness of these things may be prompted by encountering resistance. An agent may become aware that he intended to *A* or that he was about to *A* *after* he encounters resistance. (Again, the awareness at issue in this chapter is report-level awareness.)

6. Libet, Gleason, Wright, and Pearl report that "the subject was asked to note and later report the time of appearance of his conscious awareness of 'wanting' to perform a given self-initiated movement. The experience was also described as an 'urge' or 'intention' or 'decision' to move, though subjects usually settled for the words 'wanting' or 'urge'" (1983, p. 627).

7. For alleged evidence of the existence of this bias, see Libet (1985, pp. 534–35) and Libet (2004, p. 128). I discuss the accuracy of subjects' reports of their initial awareness of *x* in chapter 6.

8. It is possible that by "the experience of wanting to move" in the passage I quoted, Wegner means consciously wanting to move.

9. For readers who are not philosophers, I point out that as I use "consistent" (following standard philosophical practice), to say that *p* is *consistent* with *q* is to say that "*p* and *q*" is not a contradiction.

10. I am not suggesting that intentionally *A*-ing *entails* intending to *A*.

11. Dean Zimmerman describes substance dualism as a theory that includes a commitment to the idea that "associated with each human person, there is a thinking thing ... not

composed of the same kinds of stuff as ... nonmental things" (2006, p. 115). Zimmerman describes the "thinking thing" as a soul, but some substance dualists prefer to use the word "mind."

12. This sentence is not an endorsement of the claim that all effective occurrent distal intentions are, at some time or other, conscious intentions.

• • •

# THREE

# Neuroscience and Causes of Action

A trio of psychologists (Haggard, Newman, and Magno 1999, p. 291) describe a 1983 article by Benjamin Libet and colleagues (Libet, Gleason et al. 1983) as "one of the most philosophically challenging papers in modern scientific psychology." A striking thesis of that article is that "the brain ... 'decides' to initiate or, at the least, prepare to initiate [certain actions] at a time before there is any reportable subjective awareness that such a decision has taken place" (p. 640; see Libet 1985, p. 536).[1] In a subsequent article, Libet pointedly asserts: "If the 'act now' process is initiated unconsciously, then conscious free will is not doing it" (2001, p. 62; see Libet 2004, p. 136).

Patrick Haggard, in his contribution to a discussion with Libet, says that "conceptual analysis could help" (Haggard and Libet 2001, p. 62). He refers specifically to conceptual differences between "will (generation of action) and choice (selection of action)" (p. 61). My conceptual focus in this chapter is on other pairs of phenomena—proximal decisions and intentions, on one hand, and their relatively proximal causes, on the other. I show not only that Libet's thesis about decisions is not warranted by his data but also that the thesis is implausible on empirical grounds. In chapter 4, I extend the critique to Libet's associated position on free will.

## 1. Libet's Studies: Data, Inferences, and Problems

In some of Libet's studies, as I mentioned in chapter 2, subjects are instructed to flex their right wrists or the fingers of their right hands whenever they wish. Electrical readings from the scalp (EEGs)—averaged over at least forty flexings for each subject—show a shift in "readiness potentials" (RPs) beginning at about 550 ms before the time at which an electromyogram shows relevant muscular motion to begin (Libet 1985, pp. 529–30). (These RPs are called "type II RPs" [p. 531]. I discuss type I RPs shortly.) Subjects are also instructed to "recall . . . the spatial clock position of a revolving spot at the time of [their] initial awareness" (p. 529) of something, $x$, that Libet variously describes as a decision, intention, urge, wanting, will, or wish to move.[2] On average, RP onset preceded what the subjects reported to be the time of their initial awareness of $x$ (time W) by 350 ms. Reported time W, then, preceded the beginning of muscle motion (a muscle burst) by about 200 ms.

TABLE 3.1. Libet's Results for Type II RPs

| −550 ms | −200 ms | 0 ms |
|---|---|---|
| RP onset | reported time W | muscle begins to move |

(As mentioned in chapter 2, Libet finds independent evidence of what he regards as an error in subjects' recall of the times at which they first become aware of sensations. Correcting for it, time W is −150 ms.)

At what point, if any, does a proximal intention to flex arise in Libet's subjects? Again, Libet, Gleason et al. write: "the brain . . . 'decides' to initiate or . . . prepare to initiate the act . . . before there is any reportable subjective awareness that such a decision has taken place" (1983, p. 640). If we ignore the second disjunct, this quotation (given its context) apparently offers the answer that a proximal intention to flex appears on the scene with RP onset, about 550 ms before the muscle burst and about 350–400 ms before the agent becomes aware of the intention (see Libet 1985, p. 539); for to decide to initiate an act is to form an intention to initiate it.[3] But are decision and intention the most suitable mental items to associate with RP onset? Again, Libet described the relevant occurrence of which the agent later becomes aware not only as a decision and the onset of an intention to move but also as the onset of an urge, wanting, and a wish to move. This leaves it open that at −550 ms, rather than acquiring an intention or making a decision of which he is not conscious, the agent instead acquires an *urge* or *desire* of which he is not conscious. It is also left open that what emerges around −550 ms is a pretty reliable causal contributor to an urge or to a proximal decision or intention.

One of this chapter's main theses is that it is much more likely that what emerges around −550 ms is a *potential cause* of a proximal intention or decision than a proximal intention or decision itself. Some of the evidence I use to support this thesis is provided by another experiment reported in Libet (1985) (and elsewhere)—a "vetoing" experiment to be described shortly. Partly on the basis of the results of this experiment, Libet proposed that "conscious volitional control may operate not to initiate the volitional process but to select and control it, either by permitting or triggering the final motor outcome of the unconsciously initiated process or by vetoing the progression to actual motor activation" (1985, p. 529; see Libet 1999, p. 54; Libet 2004, pp. 139–49). "In a veto, the later phase of cerebral motor processing would be blocked, so that actual activation of the motoneurons to the muscles would not occur" (Libet 1985, p. 537).

Libet offered two kinds of evidence to support the suggestion about vetoing. One kind is generated by an experiment in which subjects are instructed to prepare to flex their fingers at a prearranged clock time and "to veto the developing intention/preparation to act ... about 100 to 200 ms before [that] time" (Libet 1985, p. 538). Subjects received both instructions at the same time. Libet writes:

> A ramplike pre-event potential was still recorded...
> resembl[ing] the RP of self-initiated acts when preplanning
> is present.... The form of the "veto" RP differed (in most
> but not all cases) from those "preset" RPs that were fol-
> lowed by actual movements [in another experiment]; the
> main negative potential tended to alter in direction (flat-
> tening or reversing) at about 150–250 ms before the preset
> time.... This difference suggests that the conscious veto
> interfered with the final development of RP processes leading
> to action.... The preparatory cerebral processes associated
> with an RP can and do develop even when intended motor
> action is vetoed at approximately the time that conscious
> intention would normally appear before a voluntary act.
> (1985, p. 538)[4]

Keep in mind that the subjects were instructed in advance
*not* to flex their fingers but to prepare to flex them at the
prearranged time and to veto this. The subjects intentionally
complied with the request. They intended from the beginning *not* to flex their fingers at the appointed time. So what is
indicated by the segment of what Libet refers to as the "veto"
RP that precedes the change of direction? Presumably, not
the presence of an *intention* to flex; for then, at some point
in time, the subjects would have both an intention to flex
at the prearranged time and an intention not to flex at that
time. And how can a normal agent simultaneously be settled
on *A*-ing at *t* and settled on not *A*-ing at *t*?[5] In short, it is
very plausible that Libet was mistaken in describing what is
vetoed as "*intended* motor action" (1985, p. 538; emphasis
added).

In some presentations I have given on Libet's work, I tell
the audience that I will count from one to five, and I ask them
to prepare to snap their fingers when I say "five" but not
to snap them. (When I hear no finger snapping, I jokingly
praise my audience for being in control of their fingers.)
Someone might suggest that these people have conscious
intentions not to flex when I get to five and unconscious

intentions to flex then and that the former intentions win out over the latter. This suggestion is simply a conjecture— an unparsimonious one—that is not backed by evidence.

A potential source of confusion should be identified. According to a common use of the expression "readiness potential" (RP), the RP is a measure of activity in the motor cortex that precedes voluntary muscle motion; by definition, averaged EEGs generated in situations in which there is no muscle burst do not count as RPs. Thus, given that there is no muscle burst in the veto experiment, some scientists would refer to what Libet calls the veto RP as an *event-related brain potential* (ERP) rather than an RP.

If the segment of the ERP in the veto scenario that precedes the change of direction is not associated with an intention to flex at the appointed time, with what might it be associated? In the passage I quoted from Libet (1985, p. 538), he compares "the 'veto' RP" with (*a*) ' "preset' RPs that were followed by actual movements" and (*b*) "the RP of self-initiated acts when preplanning is present." The RP referred to in *a* is produced in experiments in which subjects are instructed to watch the clock and flex when the revolving spot reaches "a pre-set 'clock time' " (Libet, Wright, and Gleason 1982, p. 325). "The subject was encouraged to try to make his movement coincide as closely as possible with the arrival of the spot at the pre-set time." The RP referred to in *b* is produced in two kinds of studies: (1) studies in which subjects instructed to flex spontaneously are not regularly encouraged to aim for spontaneity (Libet et al. 1982, pp. 324–26), and (2) studies in which subjects who did receive such encouragement reported that they experienced "some 'pre-planning,' " even if only in "a minority of the 40 self-initiated acts that occurred in the series for that averaged RP" (p. 328). "Even when some pre-plannings were recalled and reported, subjects insisted that the more specific urge or intention to actually move did not arise in that pre-planning stage" (p. 329). Reports of preplanning seem to include reports of thoughts about when to flex and reports of anticipations of flexing (pp. 328–29). Libet and coauthors remark, "Subject S.B. described his advance feelings [of preplanning] as 'pre-tensions' rather than pre-plannings to act" (p. 329). This subject may have meant that he occasionally experienced tension that he expected to result in flexing.

The RPs referred to in *a* and *b* have a very similar form (Libet et al. 1982, pp. 330, 333–34; Libet 1985, p. 532). RPs with that form are called "type I RPs" (Libet et al. 1982, p. 326). They have significantly earlier onsets than the RPs produced in studies of subjects regularly encouraged to aim for spontaneity who report that they experienced no preplanning—type II RPs. Again, the form of the veto RP is the form of type I RPs until "about 150–250 ms before the preset time" (Libet 1985, p. 538). What does the veto group (group V) have in common until that time with the three kinds of subjects who produce type I RPs: those with a preset time for flexing (group PS), those who are not regularly encouraged to aim for spontaneity (group N), and those who are regularly encouraged to aim for spontaneity but report some preplanning (group PP)?

Presumably, subjects in group PS are watching the clock with the intention of flexing at the preset time. But it certainly does not follow from that together with the similar RPs in groups N and PP and the similar ERP in group V for a time that members of each of these groups are watching the clock with a similar intention to flex. For one thing, as I have explained, it is very likely that group V—subjects instructed in advance to prepare to flex and then veto the preparation—are watching the clock *without* an intention to flex at the targeted time. Given that the members of group V lack this intention, we should look for something that groups V and PS actually have in common that might be signified by the similarity between the veto RP and the type I RP until about 150–250 ms before the preset time. One possibility is that during the period in question, members of both groups undergo brain events of a kind suitable for playing an important role in generating more direct causes of flexings and these events are associated with the portion at issue of the veto RP and the type I RP.[6] In the case of group V, perhaps a subject's wanting to comply with the instructions—including the instruction to prepare to flex at the appointed time—along with his or her recognition that the time is approaching produces an unconscious urge to flex soon, a pretty reliable causal contributor to an urge to flex soon, or the motor preparedness typically associated with such an urge. Things of these kinds are potential causal contributors to the acquisition of proximal intentions to flex. A related possibility is suggested by the observation that "the pattern of brain activity associated with imagining making a movement is very similar to the pattern of activity associated with preparing to make a movement" (Spence and Frith 1999, p. 27; also see Caldara et al. 2004; Ehrsson, Geyer, and Naito 2003; Jankelowitz and Colebatch 2002).[7] The instructions given to group V would naturally elicit imagining flexing very soon, an event of a kind suitable, in the circumstances, for making a causal contribution to the emergence of a proximal urge to flex. Finally, the "flattening or reversing" of the veto RP at about 150–250 ms before the preset time might indicate a consequence of the subject's vetoing his or her preparation.

What about groups N and PP? It is possible that they, along with the subjects in groups PS and V, begin acquiring urges to flex—or begin to imagine flexing very soon—at a greater temporal distance from 0 ms than do subjects encouraged to flex spontaneously who report no preplanning. That difference may be indicated by type I RPs having significantly earlier onsets than type II RPs. Another possibility is consistent with this. I have distinguished proximal from distal intentions, and Libet also recognizes the distinction (see Libet et al. 1982, pp. 329, 334; Libet 1989, pp. 183–84). Presumably, subjects in group PS respond to the instruction to flex at a preset time with an intention to flex at that time. This is a distal intention. As the preset time for flexing draws very near, that intention may help produce a proximal intention to flex, an intention to *flex now* (see Libet 1989, p. 183; Libet 1999, p. 54; Libet 2004, p. 148). That may happen around the time the ERP for group V begins to diverge from the type I RP or closer to 0 ms. And it may happen at or around the time subjects in groups N and PP acquire a proximal intention to flex. They may acquire such an intention without having had a distal intention to flex soon: recall that members of group V probably had no distal intention to flex and that their ERPs are very similar to the RPs of groups N, PP, and PS until about 150–250 ms before the preset time. All this is consistent with the similarities in the electrical readings for the various groups of subjects, on the assumption that no segment of the RPs before about −150 to 250 ms for subjects in group PS specifically represents subjects' distal intentions to flex at the preset time, even though those intentions are present. These distal intentions may be associated with an RP segment of a kind that also is associated with items of an alternative kind suitable for producing proximal intentions to flex. If so, the presence of the RP segment does not ensure that a distal intention to flex is present.

The main difference between type I and type II RPs, in Haggard's words, is that the former have "earlier onsets than" the latter (Haggard and Libet 2001, p. 49). The earlier onsets may be correlated with an earlier onset of one or more items in what I dub the *preproximal-intention group*, or PPG— namely, urges to (prepare to) flex soon, brain events suitable for being relatively proximal causal contributors to such urges, motor preparation, and motor imagery, including imagery associated with imagining flexing very soon. Items in the PPG may be brought on variously by the instruction to flex at a preset time (group PS), the instruction to prepare to flex at a preset time and veto that later (group V), unsolicited conscious thoughts about when to flex (groups N and PP), or unsolicited conscious anticipations of flexing (groups N and PP). Alternatively, these unsolicited conscious thoughts and anticipations may *be*—or be manifestations of—PPG items, rather than being elicitors of such items. These conscious PPG inciters and PPG elements are absent in subjects encouraged to flex spontaneously who report no preplanning—at least, if the subjects are not mistaken. If some segments of type I RPs indicate the presence of items in the PPG, or the presence of such items together with proximal intentions that emerge significantly later than the PPG items do, the same may be true of similar segments of type II RPs. The difference in the two kinds of RP may mainly be a matter of when some PPG item emerges—that is, how long before 0 ms.

If RP onset in cases of "spontaneous" flexing indicates the emergence of a potential cause of a proximal intention to flex, the proximal intention itself may emerge at some point between RP onset and time W, *at* time W, or *after* time W: at time W the agent may be aware only of something—a proximal urge to flex, for example—that has not yet issued in a proximal intention. Again, Libet asserts, "In a veto, the later phase of cerebral motor processing would be blocked, so that actual activation of the motoneurons to the muscles would not occur" (1985, p. 537). Perhaps in nonveto cases, activation of these motoneurons is the direct result of the acquisition of a proximal intention (Gomes 1999, pp. 68, 72; Mele 1997, pp. 322–24). Libet suggests that this activation event occurs between 10 and 90 ms before the muscle burst and apparently favors an answer in the 10–50 ms range (1985, p. 537). Elsewhere he asserts that the activation event can occur no later than 50 ms before the onset of muscle motion (Libet 2004, pp. 137–38).

For my purposes, what is of special interest are the relative times of the emergence of three things. The first is a potential relatively proximal *cause* of a proximal intention to flex. I call it a *potential PI cause*. I have speculated about what this item might be. The second is a proximal intention to flex. The third is consciousness of the intention. If RP onset indicates the emergence of a potential *PI* cause, and if acquisitions of corresponding intentions directly activate the motoneurons to the relevant muscles, we have the following picture of subjects encouraged to flex spontaneously who report no preplanning—subjects who produce type II RPs.

TABLE 3.2. A Possibility Regarding Type II RPs

    a. −550 ms: potential PI cause emerges.
    b. −90 to −50 ms: acquisition of proximal intention.[8]
    c. 0 ms: muscle begins to move.

Possibly, the intention is *consciously* acquired (see chapter 2). My point here is simply that the possibility represented in table 3.2 is *consistent* with Libet's data on type II RPs and on time W.[9]

In an alternative picture, the acquisition of a proximal intention to flex sends a signal that may be regarded as a command to flex one's wrist (or finger), and that signal helps produce finer-grained signals that directly activate the motoneurons to the relevant muscles. This picture moves the time of the acquisition of a proximal intention further from 0 ms, but it does not move it anywhere near −550 ms, as I explain in section 2.

I mentioned that Libet offered a second kind of evidence for veto control. Subjects encouraged to flex "spontaneously" (in nonveto experiments) "reported that during some of the trials a recallable conscious urge to act appeared but was 'aborted' or somehow suppressed before any actual movement occurred; in such cases the subject simply waited for another urge to appear, which, when consummated, constituted the actual event whose RP was recorded" (1985, p. 538). (No record was made of electrical activity for suppressed urges. I explain why in chapter 4.) Notice that it is *urges* that these subjects are said here to report and abort or suppress.[10] In group V (the veto group), as I have explained, there is excellent reason to believe that no proximal *intention* to flex is present, and the ERPs for this group resembled the type I RPs for these other three groups until about 150–250 ms before the preset time. If it is assumed that these averaged EEGs represent the same thing for these four groups until those for group V diverge from the others, these averaged EEGs probably do *not* represent a proximal intention to flex before the point of divergence, but they might represent a potential causal contributor to an urge to (prepare to) flex or other items in the PPG. And if at least until about the time of divergence there is no proximal intention to flex in any of these groups, we would need a special reason to believe that the type II RPs of the spontaneous flexers indicate that proximal intentions to flex emerge in them around −550 ms. In section 2, I show that there is independent evidence that their proximal intentions emerge much closer to 0 ms than this.

Does the brain decide to initiate actions "at a time before there is any reportable subjective awareness that such a decision has taken place" (Libet, Gleason et al. 1983, p. 640)? Libet and colleagues certainly have not shown that it does, for their data do not show that any such decision has been made before time W or before the time at which their subjects first are aware of a *decision* or *intention* to flex. Nothing justifies the claim that what a subject becomes aware of at time W is a *decision* to flex that has already been made or an *intention* to flex that has already been acquired, as opposed, for example, to something in the PPG. Indeed, the data about vetoing, as I have explained, can reasonably be used to argue that the potential PI cause hypothesis about what the RPs indicate is less implausible than the decision or intention hypothesis. Now there certainly seems to be a connection between what happens at −550 ms and subsequent muscle motion in cases of spontaneous flexing. But it obviously is not a temporally direct connection. Between the former and latter times, subjects apparently form or acquire proximal intentions to flex, in those cases in which they do intentionally flex. For all Libet's data show, those intentions may be consciously formed or acquired.

In chapter 2, I mentioned my own experience as a subject in an experiment like Libet's. Naturally, I do not want to make much of that here: I am only one subject, after all, and I might not be a representative one. At first, my plan was to wait to experience something in the ballpark of an urge or an intention to flex and then flex in response to it. But because I had no such experiences, I hit on the strategy I mentioned: silently saying "now!" to myself (and then flexing straightaway). This, as I mentioned, was the conscious event that I tried to keep track of with the assistance of the clock; and I thought of the "now!" as shorthand for the imperative "flex now!"—a self-command. I am on record as a defender of the view that there are no uncaused actions (Mele 2003), and my silent sayings of "now!" to myself were actions— mental ones—as were my flexings. Perhaps items in the PPG were among the causes of my self-commands and the subsequent flexings, and perhaps issuing the self-commands was my way of forming proximal intentions to flex. Whatever the relatively proximal causes of my proximal intentions to flex were, they were not themselves proximal intentions to flex. And it may be that no proximal intention to flex— as opposed to potential *causes* of such an intention—was present in me before I said "now!," something I *consciously* did.

## 2. A Test: Reaction Times

I have offered some grounds for holding that the potential PI cause hypothesis about what the onset of type II RPs indicates in Libet's studies is less implausible than the decision or intention hypothesis. Is there an independent way to test these hypotheses—that is, to gather evidence about whether it is potential PI causes that emerge around −550 ms in Libet's studies or instead decisions or intentions? One line of thought runs as follows. (1) All overt intentional actions are caused by decisions (or intentions); (2) the type II RPs, which emerge around −550 ms, are correlated with causes of the flexing actions (because they regularly precede the onset of muscle motion); so (3) these RPs indicate that decisions are made (or intentions acquired) at −550 ms. I have shown that this line of thought is unpersuasive. A lot can happen in a causal process that runs for 550 ms, including a PPG item making a causal contribution to a subject's proximally deciding to flex (or acquiring a proximal intention to flex). One can reply that even so, 3 *might* be true. And, of course, I can run through my argumentation about the veto and related matters again to remind the imaginary respondent why 3 is improbable. But what about a test?

If makings of proximal decisions to flex or acquisitions of proximal intentions to flex (or the physical events that realize these things) cause muscle motion, how long does it take them to do that? Does it take about 550 ms? Might reaction time experiments show that 550 ms is too long a time for this? Some caution is in order here. In typical reaction time experiments, subjects have decided in advance to perform an assigned task—to A, for short—whenever they detect the relevant signal. When they detect the signal, there is no need for a proximal *decision* to A.[11] (If all decisions are responses to uncertainty about what to do and subjects are not uncertain about what to do when they detect the signal, there is no place here for proximal decisions to A.[12]) However, it is plausible that after they detect the signal, they acquire a proximal *intention* to A. That is, it is plausible that the combination of their conditional intention to A when they detect the signal (or the physical correlate of that intention) and their detection of the signal (or the physical correlate of that detection) produces a proximal intention to $A$. The acquisition of this intention (or the physical correlate of that event) would then initiate the $A$-ing.[13] And in a reaction time experiment (described shortly) in which subjects are watching a Libet clock, the time between the go signal and the onset of muscle motion is much shorter than 550 ms. This is evidence that proximal intentions to flex—as opposed to items in the PPG—emerge much closer to the time of the onset of muscle motion than 550 ms. There is no reason, in principle, that it should take people any longer to start flexing their wrists when executing a proximal intention to flex in Libet's studies than it takes them to do so when executing such an intention in a reaction time study. More precisely, there is no reason, in principle, that the interval between proximal intention acquisition and the beginning of muscle motion should be significantly different in the two scenarios.[14]

The line of reasoning I have just sketched depends on the assumption that in reaction time studies, proximal intentions to $A$ are at work. An alternative possibility is that the combination of subjects' conditional intentions to $A$ when they detect the signal and their detection of the signal initiates the $A$-ing without there being any proximal intention to $A$. Of course, if this is possible, there is a parallel possibility in the case of Libet's subjects. Perhaps, on many occasions, the combination of their conditional intentions to flex when they next feel like it—conscious intentions, presumably— together with relevant feelings (for example, felt urges to flex soon) initiates a flexing in the absence of any proximal intentions to flex. (They may treat their initial consciousness of the urge as a go signal, as suggested in Keller and Heckhausen 1990, p. 352.) If that possibility is an actuality, then on these occasions, Libet's thesis is false, of course: there is no intention to flex "now" on these occasions—in which case no such intention is produced by the brain before the mind is aware of it. (In my own case, my conditional intention to flex whenever I said "now!" together with a "now!" saying may have initiated a flexing without the assistance of a proximal intention to flex. I may have misinterpreted my silent speech acts as expressions of decisions, and they might have functioned instead simply as go signals.)

The reaction time study I mentioned is reported in Haggard and Magno (1999):

> Subjects sat at a computer watching a clock hand...whose rotation period was 2.56 s....After an unpredictable delay, varying from 2.56 to 8 s, a high-frequency tone...was played over a loudspeaker. This served as a warning stimulus for the subsequent reaction. 900 ms after the warning stimulus onset, a second tone...was played. [It] served as the go signal. Subjects were instructed to respond as rapidly as possible to the go signal with a right-key press on a computer mouse button. Subjects were instructed not to anticipate the go stimulus and were reprimanded if they responded on catch trials. (p. 103)

The endpoints of reaction times, as calculated in this study, are the sounding of the go signal and "the EMG signal for the onset of the first sustained burst of muscle activity occurring after the go signal" (p. 104). "Reaction time" here, then, starts *before* any intention to press "now" is acquired: obviously, it takes some time to detect the signal, and if detection of the signal helps produce a proximal intention, that takes some time, too. The mean of the subjects' median reaction times in the control trials was 231 ms (p. 104). If a proximal intention to press was acquired, that happened, on average, nearer to the time of muscle motion than 231 ms and therefore much nearer than the 550 ms that Libet claims is the time proximal intentions to flex are unconsciously acquired in his studies. Notice also how close we are getting to Libet's subjects' average reported time of their initial awareness of something he variously describes as an intention, urge, wanting, decision, will, or wish to move (reported time W: −200 ms). If proximal intentions to flex are acquired in Libet's studies, Haggard and Magno's results make it look like a better bet that they are acquired on average around reported time W than around −550 ms.[15] How seriously we should take Libet's subjects' reports of the time of their initial awareness of the urge, intention, or whatever, is a controversial question. I reserve discussion of it for chapter 6.

Recall Haggard's assertion that "conceptual analysis could help" (Haggard and Libet 2001, p. 62). Parts of this chapter may be read as a test of his assertion. In my opinion, the result is positive. Attention not only to the data but also to the concepts in terms of which the data are analyzed makes it clear that Libet's striking claims about decisions and intentions are not justified by his results. The next chapter provides additional support for this conclusion.

#### NOTES

1. In a later article, Libet writes: "the brain has begun the specific preparatory processes for the voluntary act well before the subject is even aware of any wish or intention to act" (1992, p. 263).

2. Some passages in which two or more of these terms are used interchangeably are quoted later in this chapter and in chapter 4.

3. I say *apparently*, because an author may wish to distinguish an intention to flex one's wrist from an intention to initiate a flexing of one's wrist. I discuss initiation in chapter 4. For completeness, I observe that if we instead ignore the quotation's first disjunct, it makes a claim about when an intention to *prepare* to flex—or to prepare to initiate a flexing of one's wrist—arises.

4. For a more thorough discussion of the experiment, see Libet, Wright, and Curtis (1983) or Libet, Gleason et al. (1983).

5. On some abnormal agents, see chapter 1, note 7.

6. Another is that they have an intention to prepare to flex, if *preparing* is understood in such a way that so intending does not entail intending to flex.

7. James Kilner and coauthors produce evidence that, as they put it, "the readiness potential (RP)—an electrophysiological marker of motor preparation—is present when one is observing someone else's action" (Kilner, Vargas, Duval, Blakemore, and Sirigu 2004, p. 1299).

8. This figure is based on Libet's suggestion that the activation event occurs between 10 and 90 ms before the onset of muscle motion (1985, p. 537) in light of his revision of the lower limit to 50 ms (2004, pp. 137–38).

9. I remind readers who are not philosophers that, as I use "consistent," to say that *p* is *consistent* with *q* is to say that "*p* and *q*" is not a contradiction.

10. In the same article, Libet asserts that subjects were "free *not* to act out any given urge or initial decision to act; and each subject indeed reported frequent instances of such aborted intentions" (p. 530).

11. It should not be assumed that detecting the signal is a conscious event (see Prinz 2003).

12. In a reaction time study in which subjects are instructed to *A* or *B* when they detect the signal and not to decide in advance which to do, they may decide between *A* and *B* after detecting the signal.

13. Hereafter, the parenthetical clauses should be supplied by the reader.

14. Notice that the interval at issue is distinct from intervals between the time of the occurrence of events that cause proximal intentions and the time of intention acquisition.

15. In a study by Day et al. of eight subjects instructed to flex a wrist when they hear a tone, mean reaction time was 125 ms (1989, p. 653). In their study of five subjects instructed to flex both wrists when they hear a tone, mean

reaction time was 93 ms (p. 658). The mean reaction times of both groups of subjects—defined as "the interval from auditory tone to onset of the first antagonist EMG burst" (p. 651)—were much shorter than those of Haggard and Magno's subjects. Day et al.'s subjects, unlike Haggard and Magno's (and Libet's), were not watching a clock.

• • •

# FOUR

# Neuroscience and Free Will

Benjamin Libet asserts that his "discovery that the brain unconsciously initiates the volitional process well before the person becomes aware of an intention or wish to act voluntarily...clearly has a profound impact on how we view the nature of free will" (2004, p. 201). In this chapter, I explain why this discovery is not all it is cracked up to be.

## 1. Action Initiation

When Libet's work is applied to the theoretically subtle and complicated issue of free will, things can quickly get out of hand. The abstract of Haggard and Libet (2001) opens as follows: "The problem of free will lies at the heart of modern scientific studies of consciousness. An influential series of experiments by Libet has suggested that conscious intentions arise as a result of brain activity. This contrasts with traditional concepts of free will, in which the mind controls the body" (p. 47). Only a certain kind of mind–body (or "substance") dualist (see chapter 2, note 11) would hold that conscious intentions do *not* "arise as a result of brain activity," and such dualist views are rarely advocated in contemporary philosophical publications on free will. Moreover, contemporary philosophers who argue for the existence of free will typically shun substance dualism. However, Libet's data and many of the conclusions

*Actions are*
*produced*
*unconsciously*
*550 msec*
*before*
*the action*

he derives from them can be separated from dualistic presuppositions.

Libet writes: "It is only the final 'act now' process that produces the voluntary *act*. That 'act now' process begins in the brain about 550 msec before the act, and it begins unconsciously" (2001, p. 61).[1] "There is," he says, "an unconscious gap of about 400 msec between the onset of the cerebral process and when the person becomes consciously aware of his/her decision or wish or intention to act." (Incidentally, a page later, he identifies what the agent becomes aware of as "the intention/wish/urge to act.") He adds: "If the 'act now' process is initiated unconsciously, then conscious free will is not doing it" (p. 61).

In chapter 3, I explained that Libet has not shown that a proximal decision to flex is made or a proximal intention to flex acquired around −550 ms in subjects who display type II RPs and that it is highly improbable that he is right about this. However, even if the proximal intention emerges much later, that is compatible with an "act now" process having begun at −550 ms. Regarding processes of many kinds, taking a position on when they begin is partly a matter of stipulation. Did the process of my baking a frozen pizza begin when I turned my oven on to preheat it, when I opened the door of the heated oven five minutes later, when I placed the pizza on the center rack, when I subsequently closed the oven door, or at some other time? Theorists can argue about this, but I prefer not to. Nor do I care to stipulate a starting point for the process. One might say that the act now process in subjects who act spontaneously and report no preplanning begins with the formation or acquisition of a proximal intention to flex, much closer to the onset of muscle motion than −550 ms, or that it begins earlier, with the beginning of a process that issues in the intention. I have no desire to argue about that. Suppose we stipulate that in these subjects, the act now process begins with the emergence of some item in what in chapter 3 I called the preproximal-intention group

(PPG) at about −550 ms and that the item plays a significant role in producing a proximal intention to flex many milliseconds later. We can then agree with Libet that given that the "process is initiated unconsciously, . . . conscious free will is not doing it"—that is, is not initiating the act now process. But should we have thought that conscious free will has the job of producing items in the PPG? In the philosophical literature, free will's primary locus of operation is typically placed elsewhere—in the act of deciding (or choosing). An example might be freely deciding not to bake a pizza after all and to turn one's preheated oven off after having initiated something that one regards as a pizza-baking process.

As the preceding example illustrates, the assertion that a process is *initiated* does not entail that it will be completed. This is a point to bear in mind. Libet himself appeals to grounds for believing that an act now process that is initiated unconsciously may be aborted by the agent and therefore not be completed. That apparently is what happens in instances of spontaneous vetoing (Libet 1985, pp. 530, 538), if act now processes start when Libet says they do.[2]

Libet asks (2001, p. 62), "How would the 'conscious self' initiate a voluntary act if, factually, the process to 'act now' is initiated unconsciously?" I offer an answer here. Processes have parts, and the various parts of a process may have more and less proximal initiators. A process that is initiated by an item in the PPG may have a subsequent part that is directly initiated by a consciously made decision. The conscious self—which need not be understood as something mysterious—might more proximally initiate a voluntary act that is less proximally initiated by an item in the PPG. Readers who, like me, prefer to use "self" only as an affix may prefer to say that the acquisition or formation of a relevant proximal intention—and specifically, an intention that is consciously acquired or formed—might more proximally initiate an intentional action that is less proximally initiated by an item in the PPG.

Recall that Libet himself says that "conscious volitional control may operate ... to select and control ['the volitional process'], either by permitting or triggering the final motor outcome of the unconsciously initiated process or by vetoing the progression to actual motor activation" (1985, p. 529). "Triggering" is a kind of initiating. In "triggering the final motor outcome," the formation or acquisition of a proximal intention would be initiating an action in a more direct way than does the PPG item that initiated a process that issued in the decision or intention.[3]

In light of the foregoing, the following inference by Susan Pockett ought to strike readers as seriously misguided. Drawing on Libet's work, Pockett writes:

> In the case of very simple voluntary acts such as pressing a button whenever one feels like it, good experimental evidence shows that the consciousness of being about to move arises before the movement occurs, but after the neural events leading up to the movement have begun. It is a reasonable conclusion that consciousness is not the immediate cause of this simple kind of behavior. (2006, p. 21)

If consciousness is a property, and if, as some philosophers maintain, it is a conceptual truth that properties themselves do not cause anything, no data are needed to support Pockett's final assertion about consciousness here. However, what she means to be asserting is that in cases of the kind in question, the agent's conscious intention to press the button is "not the immediate cause" of his button-pressing. And the reason she offers for accepting this claim is that "the neural events leading up to the movement" begin before a conscious intention emerges. But this observation about neural events is entirely consistent with it being true that these events are among the more remote causes of an action that has the acquisition of a conscious proximal intention among its less remote causes—in which case, of course, the earlier neural events definitely are *not* the *immediate* cause of the action, whereas the acquisition of the conscious intention might be.

Of course, even if the acquisition of the conscious intention is a less remote cause of the action, it is a further question whether the intention plays a role in producing the action that depends on it being a *conscious* intention (see chapter 2), an issue I return to in chapter 7. The point to be noticed here is that from the datum that some "neural events leading up to the movement" begin before a conscious proximal intention emerges, one cannot legitimately infer that any of the following play no role in producing the movement: the acquisition of the proximal intention, the agent's consciousness of the intention, or the physical correlates of either of these items. After all, when lighting a  fuse precedes the burning of the fuse, which in turn precedes a firecracker exploding, we do not infer that the burning of the fuse plays no causal role in producing the explosion. If Pockett is thinking that the earlier neural events are part of a neural process that would have resulted in a button-pressing even if the agent had not acquired a conscious proximal intention to press the button, she should say so and produce supporting evidence.[4] For all she says, the neural events that precede the emergence of a conscious intention in these studies may be intrinsically indistinguishable from neural events that occur in cases in which Libet's subjects spontaneously veto conscious urges and then wait for a subsequent urge before flexing. (I return to this possibility shortly.) If that is so, the occurrence of these neural events leaves it open whether the agent will or will not flex very soon and open that he would not have flexed about half a second later if he had not acquired a conscious proximal intention to flex before flexing.

Pockett is not alone in reasoning in the fallacious way just discussed. Henry Roediger and coauthors write: "Clearly conscious intention cannot cause an action if a neural event that precedes and correlates with the action comes before conscious intention" (Roediger, Goode, and Zaromb 2008, p. 208). Azim Shariff and coauthors make a similar claim: "Libet and colleagues found that what they identified to be the volitional impulse to begin the action occurred around 350 ms *after* the readiness potential had begun. Without temporal primacy, it is very difficult to attribute causation to the volitional impulse" (2008, p. 186). But, obviously, not only is there no rule against causes themselves having causes, it also is the *norm* for causes to have causes. (How many causal processes start with uncaused causes?)

Patrick Haggard makes a faulty inference from the data produced by Libet's main experiment that resembles Pockett's faulty inference. He writes: "The seminal studies of Benjamin Libet ... suggested that conscious intention occurs *after* the onset of preparatory brain activity. It cannot therefore cause our actions, as a cause cannot occur after its effect" (2005, p. 291). One might think that Haggard is claiming that conscious intention cannot cause actions because it occurs after the actions with which it is associated. But he is not. Haggard finds it plausible that in these studies, conscious intentions arise before the associated actions (2006, p. 83; see Haggard 2005, p. 291). His claim is that because "conscious intention occurs after the onset of *preparatory brain activity*" (emphasis changed), it "cannot ... cause our actions" (2005, p. 291).

William Banks's reasoning resembles Pockett's and Haggard's. He writes: "The clear implication ... is that the conscious decision was not the cause of the action" (2006, p. 237). Banks also reports that although "the most common" view, which he propounds, "is that the unconscious process as measured by the RP is sufficient in and of itself to initiate action—and the conscious decision is an ineffective latecomer, along for the ride," this view should be tested (p. 239). He asserts that for the common view "to be verified, we need an absence of cases in which RP potentials are found but do not eventuate in the response," and, he adds,

> It is possible that robust RPs crop up frequently during the critical interval, but only when conscious decision is reported is there a response. In this case the unconscious process would clearly not be a sufficient cause of the action. We do not detect the ineffective RPs because recording RPs requires back-averaging from the response. The RPs that do not eventuate in a response would therefore not be discovered.

Two points should be made straightaway. First, in the sense in which Banks is using "RPs" here (according to which it is not true by definition that there are no RPs without muscle bursts), it is false that recording RPs *requires* back-averaging from a muscle burst. (Back-averaging from muscle bursts involves using muscle bursts to trigger the making of a record of preceding brain activity.) Recall that EEGs (what Libet calls the veto RP) were recorded for subjects instructed to prepare to flex at *t* but not to flex then. The EEGs were back-averaged from *t*, and, as I mentioned in chapter 3, they resembled type I RPs until "about 150–250 ms before" *t* (Libet 1985, p. 538)—until *time v*, for short. Second, this is evidence that the brain events indicated by the segment of the type I RPs that precedes time *v* are not sufficient for producing a flexing—and, more precisely, that they are not sufficient for producing events that are sufficient for producing a flexing (that is, less distant sufficient causes). If (1) until time *v*, the veto RP and the type I RPs are produced by neural events of the same kind, then (2) the occurrence of events of that kind is not sufficient for producing (events that are sufficient for producing) a flexing. For if 1 is true and 2 were false, the subjects in the veto experiment would have flexed.

I return to the shorter, type II RPs exhibited by the subjects in Libet's main study. How tightly connected is the brain activity registered by, say, the first 300 ms of these RPs—call it *type 300 activity*—to subsequent flexings? Is it as tightly connected to flexings as lightings of firecracker fuses are to firecracker explosions? In fact, no one knows. In this study, the muscle burst triggers a computer to make a record of the preceding brain activity. In the absence of a muscle burst, no record is made for the purposes of back-averaging. For all anyone knows, there were many occasions in which type 300 activity occurred in Libet's subjects and there was no associated flexing. Type 300 activity may raise the probability that a muscle burst will occur at about 0 ms without raising it anywhere near 1, and it may be at most a potential causal contributor to such a muscle burst.

In cases in which subjects reported spontaneous vetoing, there was no back-averaging—for the reason just mentioned. As Libet points out, "In the absence of the muscle's electrical signal when being activated, there was no trigger to initiate the computer's recording of any RP that may have preceded the veto" (2004, p. 141). So, for all anyone knows, there was, in these cases, electrical activity that matched type I or type II RPs until the veto. Moreover, what is vetoed, rather than being a decision that was unconsciously made or an intention that was unconsciously acquired, might have been a conscious urge. (Again, "urge" was the spontaneous vetoers' preferred term.)

Daniel Dennett echoes a common judgment when he asserts that the type II RP is "a highly reliable predictor" of flexing (2003, p. 229). Even if this is true of the entire type II RP, it is not known whether this is true of, say, its first 300 ms segment, as I have just explained. Not only is it highly implausible that the beginning of a type II RP indicates the making of a proximal decision or the acquiring of a proximal intention (see chapter 3), it also is unknown how tight the connection is between type 300 activity and action. No one has shown (*S1*) that type 300 activity is sufficient to produce (events that are sufficient for producing) a muscle burst around 0 ms. Nor has anyone shown (*S2*) that *S1* would be true if not for the possibility of a conscious veto. Those who believe that one or the other of these propositions has been shown to be true either do not realize that in the experiments that yield Libet's type II RPs, the "muscle's electrical signal when being activated" is what triggers the computer to make a record of the preceding brain activity for the purposes of averaging (Libet 2004, p. 141) or do not recognize the implications of this. How can we, on the basis of the data, be justified in believing that type 300 activity has the actual or counterfactual "sufficiency" at issue, if no one has looked to see whether type 300 activity is ever present in cases in which there is no muscle burst around 0 ms? The answer is simple: we cannot.[5]

In chapter 2, I mentioned the possibility that some of Libet's subjects may interpret their instructions as including an instruction to wait until they experience an urge to flex before they flex and to flex in response to that experience. Another possibility is that some subjects treat the conscious urge as what may be called a *decide signal*—a signal calling for them consciously to decide right then whether to flex right away or to wait a while. It may be claimed that by the time the conscious urge emerges, it is too late for the subject to refrain from acting on it (something that Libet denies) and that is why the conscious urge should not be seen as part of the action-causing process, even if subjects think they are treating the urge as a go or decide signal.[6] One way to get evidence about this is to conduct an experiment in which subjects are instructed to flex at time *t* *unless* they detect a stop signal. (For a users' guide on stop-signal experiments, see Logan 1994.) In this way, by varying the interval between the stop signal and *t*, experimenters can try to ascertain when subjects reach the point of no return. (Naturally, in most trials there should be no stop signal.) Perhaps it will be discovered that that point is reached significantly later than time W. (Of course, some researchers and theorists worry about how seriously subjects' reports of their first awareness of a proximal urge or intention to flex should be taken. On this issue, see chapter 6.)

Time $t$ can be a designated point on a Libet clock, and brain activity can be measured backward from $t$. My guess is that in trials in which there is no stop signal, subjects will produce something resembling a type I RP. In trials in which a subject reacts to the stop signal by refraining from flexing at $t$, he might display averaged EEGs that resemble what Libet calls "the 'veto' RP" (1985, p. 538). Although there is a large literature on stop signal studies, I have found no reports on experiments of the sort just sketched. If I had a neuroscience lab, I would conduct the experiment.

## 2. More on Vetoing

A recent study by Marcel Brass and Patrick Haggard (2007) has an apparent bearing on some of the issues discussed here and in chapter 3. Partly because the study may seem to generate some good neuroscientific news about free will, it merits attention here. Discussion of the study also affords me the opportunity to highlight a certain noteworthy difficulty encountered in experimental studies of the vetoing of proximal urges, intentions, or decisions.

Brass and Haggard conduct an experiment in which subjects are "instructed to freely decide when to execute a key press while observing a rotating clock hand" on a Libet-like clock and "to cancel the intended response at the last possible moment in some trials that they freely selected" (2007, pp. 9141–42). They report that "the mean proportion of inhibition trials was 45.5%, but that there were large interindividual differences, with the proportion of inhibition trials ranging from 28 to 62%" and that "subjects reported the subjective experience of deciding to initiate action a mean of −141 ms before the key press on action trials"

(p. 9142). If the subjects actually did what Brass and Haggard say they were instructed to do, they vetoed their decisions an average of 45.5 percent of the time.

In light of Brass and Haggard's results, should everyone now grant that Libet was right—that people have time to veto conscious proximal decisions or intentions? Naturally, some researchers will worry that "in inhibition trials," subjects were *simulating* vetoing conscious proximal decisions rather than actually making conscious proximal decisions to press that they proceeded to veto. A reasonable question to ask in this connection is what strategy subjects thought they were adopting for complying with the instructions. There are various possibilities, and four of nineteen subjects in a "pre-experiment" were excluded from the actual experiment because they "reported that they were not able to follow the instructions" (2007, p. 9141). Apparently, these subjects failed to hit on a strategy that they deemed satisfactory for complying with the instructions. What strategies might the other fifteen subjects have used?

Here is one hypothetical strategy.

*Strategy 1.* On each trial, consciously decide in advance to *prepare* to press the key when the rotating clock hand hits a certain point $p$ on the clock, but leave it open whether, when the hand hits $p$, I will consciously decide to press right then or consciously decide not to press on that trial. On some trials, when the hand hits $p$, decide right then to press at once; and on some other trials decide right then not to press. Pick different $p$ points on different trials.[7]

Subjects who execute this strategy as planned do not actually veto conscious proximal decisions to press. In fact, they do not veto any conscious decisions. Their first conscious decision on each trial is to *prepare* to press a bit later, when the hand hits point $p$. They do not veto this decision; they do *prepare* to press at that time. Nor do they veto a subsequent conscious decision. If, when they think the hand reaches $p$, they consciously decide to press, they press; and if, at that point, they consciously decide not to press, they do not press. (Inattentive readers may wonder why I think I know all this. I know it because, by hypothesis, the imagined subjects *execute strategy 1 as planned*.)

A second strategy is more streamlined.

> *Strategy 2.* On some trials, consciously decide to press the key and then execute that decision at once. On other trials, consciously decide not to press the key and do not press it.

Subjects who execute this strategy as planned do not veto any conscious decisions.

Here is a third strategy.

> *Strategy 3.* On some trials, consciously decide to press the key a bit later and execute that decision. On other trials, consciously decide to press the key a bit later but do not execute that decision; instead, veto (cancel, retract) the decision.

Any subjects who execute this strategy as planned do veto some conscious decisions, but the decisions they veto are not proximal decisions. Instead, they are decisions to press *a bit later*. A subject may define "a bit later" in terms of some preselected point on the clock or leave the notion vague.

The final hypothetical strategy to be considered is even more ambitious.

> *Strategy 4.* On some trials, consciously decide to "press now" and execute that decision at once. On other trials, consciously decide to "press now" but do not execute that decision; instead, immediately veto (cancel, retract) the decision.

If any subjects execute the fourth strategy as planned, they do veto some conscious proximal decisions. Of course, we are faced with the question whether this strategy is actually executable. Do subjects have enough time to prevent themselves from executing a conscious proximal decision to press? In a real-world scenario, an agent might proximally decide to *A* and then detect something that warrants retracting the decision. For example, a quarterback might proximally decide to throw a pass to a certain receiver and then detect the threat of an interception. Perhaps he has time to veto his decision in light of this new information. The situation of the subjects in the experiment under consideration is very different. They never detect anything that warrants retracting their arbitrary decisions. If they were to retract their arbitrary decisions, they would *arbitrarily* retract them. This is quite unlike the nonarbitrary imagined vetoing by the quarterback.[8]

I asked whether Brass and Haggard's subjects can prevent themselves from executing conscious proximal decisions to press. The results of their experiment leave this question unanswered. If we knew that some subjects were successfully using strategy 4, we would have an answer. What would knowing that require? Possibly, if asked about their strategy during debriefing, some subjects would describe it as I have described strategy 4. However, that alone would not give us the knowledge at issue. People are often wrong about how they do things.

## 3. Free Will and the Liberty of Indifference

As some philosophers conceive of free will (Campbell 1957, pp. 167–74; Kane 1989, p. 252; van Inwagen 1989), exercises of it can occur only in situations in which people make significant moral or practical decisions in the face of temptation or competing motivation. This obviously is a far cry from picking a moment at which to begin one's next flexing action in Libet's study. However, other philosophers are much less restrictive about free will (Clarke 2003, chap. 7; Fischer and Ravizza 1992; O'Connor 2000, pp. 101–107). In instances of what has been called "the liberty of indifference," agents are, in Robert Kane's words, "equally attracted to more than one option" (1996, p. 108). For example, an agent may be equally attracted to each member of a pair of alternatives on a breakfast menu—an egg bagel and a sesame bagel, say. Arguably, an agent may freely choose one of the two items even though nothing important hinges on his choice. The choice of a moment to begin flexing from among an array of very similar moments is perhaps similar enough to a choice of a bagel in an instance of the liberty of indifference that people who are inclined to see the latter choice as possibly free may have the same inclination about the former choice. On a latitudinarian conception of free will that countenances the possibility of free action in the sphere of the liberty of indifference, Libet's studies may have some bearing on free will.

Unfortunately, the bearing of Libet's results on the question of whether people ever exercise free will has been seriously misunderstood. A striking illustration of this in provided by V. S. Ramachandran, who proposes the following thought experiment:

> I'm monitoring your EEG while you wiggle your finger. . . . I will see a readiness potential a second before you act. But suppose I display the signal on a screen in front of you so that you can *see* your free will. Every time you are about to wiggle your finger, supposedly using your own free will, the machine will tell you a second in advance! (2004, p. 87)

Ramachandran asks what you would experience, and he offers the following answer:

> There are three logical possibilities. (1) You might experience a sudden loss of will, feeling that the machine is controlling you, that you are a mere puppet and that free will is just an illusion. . . . (2) You might think that it does not change your sense of free will one iota, preferring to believe that the machine has some sort of spooky paranormal precognition by which it is able to predict your movements

accurately. (3) You might ... deny the evidence of your eyes and maintain that your sensation of will preceded the machine's signal.

This list of possibilities is not exhaustive. Here is another: you might experience an urge to test the machine's powers, and you might wonder whether you can watch for the signal to appear on the screen and intentionally refrain from wiggling your finger for a minute or two after you see it. Libet's data definitely leave it open that you can do this. You might even display an EEG that resembles the ERP displayed by Libet's subjects in the veto experiment (the veto RP). Perhaps you hit on the imagined test because it occurs to you that (1) "whenever you wiggle your finger, signal $S$ appears a second before you wiggle it" does not entail (2) "whenever signal $S$ appears, you wiggle your finger a second later." (A brain event signified by signal $S$ may be causally necessary for your wiggling your finger without causally ensuring that you will wiggle it. Incidentally, whenever Lydia wins a lottery prize, she buys a lottery ticket before she wins; but to her dismay, it is false that whenever she buys a lottery ticket, she wins a lottery prize.) If you succeed in your watch-and-refrain attempt, you might have the further thought that $S$ is a sign of the presence of a potential cause of a proximal intention or decision to wiggle your finger and that, even when that potential cause is present, you may decide not to wiggle your finger and behave accordingly. But if this is how you are thinking, then, provided that you are thinking clearly, you will not see the machine as controlling you. And clear thinker that you are, you will neither be tempted to believe that the machine has paranormal predictive powers nor moved to deny the evidence of your eyes.

Some readers may be inclined to suggest that if subjects' proximal decisions to flex have among their relatively proximal causes items of which the subjects are not conscious, then these decisions and the subsequent flexings are not exercises of the subjects' "free will." Some such readers may worry that this suggestion is generalizable to all decisions. Attention to Libet's response to a related suggestion helps set the stage for my discussion of this worry.

In Libet's view, consciousness opens a tiny window of opportunity for free will in his subjects. He contends that after a subject becomes conscious of his proximal intention to flex, he can freely veto the intention (1999; 2004, pp. 137–49). If the person becomes aware of his intention at $-150$ ms, and if by $-50$ ms his condition is such that "the act goes to completion with no possibility of its being stopped by the rest of the cerebral cortex" (Libet 2004, p. 138), his window of opportunity is open for 100 ms. Libet writes: "The role of conscious free will [is] not to initiate a voluntary act, but rather to control whether the act takes place. We may view the unconscious initiatives as 'bubbling up' in the brain. The conscious-will then selects which of these initiatives may go forward to an action or which ones to veto and abort" (1999, p. 54).

Libet discusses "the possibility that the conscious veto itself may have its origin in preceding unconscious processes, just as is the case for the development and appearance of the conscious will" (1999, p. 52). If having such an origin renders the proximal decision to flex unfree and the (decision to) veto has an origin of the same kind, its origin would seem to render it unfree. Libet contends that although "factors on which the decision to veto...is *based*" may "develop by unconscious processes that precede the veto...the *conscious decision to veto* could still be made without direct specification for that decision by the preceding unconscious processes" (1999, p. 53). He also asserts that the "decision to veto" might not "require preceding unconscious processes" (1999, p. 53).

It is not clear what Libet has in mind here. He may be suggesting that although free decisions to veto have unconscious processes among their causes, these decisions are not deterministically caused, and he may be suggesting that free decisions to veto are not causally dependent on "preceding unconscious processes."[9] (Actually, he seems to be making both claims.) Whatever Libet's view on this may be, one should ask how worrisome is the worry he is addressing.

Sometimes agents are indifferent between or among their leading options. Buridan's ass was in that situation regarding two equally attractive bales of hay, and scenarios of the kind at issue are sometimes referred to as "Buridan scenarios."[10] Al, whose shopping list includes a half-pound jar of Carl's Cashews, is in a position of this kind regarding the nearest jars in the Carl's Cashews array he is facing in the supermarket. And subjects in Libet's main experiment are in this position regarding various moments to begin flexing. One difference between the latter two cases is that Al has been in many Buridan situations in supermarkets, whereas Libet's subjects, at least for a time, are unaccustomed to the task of picking a moment to begin flexing from an array of moments. A related difference is that owing to the experimental design, Libet's subjects' moment-picking task is salient for them—after all, they have to report on when they first became aware of an urge or intention to flex—whereas Al's cashew-picking task is far from salient for him. Al's taking jar $X$ from the array would seem to have at least part of "its origin in preceding unconscious processes." Although he remembers that a half-pound jar of Carl's Cashews is on his shopping list and is conscious of an array of cashews and of grabbing a jar and putting it in his shopping cart, his taking the particular jar he takes—jar $X$—is not explained by any conscious decision on his part to take that jar nor by any conscious preference for that jar. Agents are well served by automatic, unconscious tie-breaking mechanisms in familiar Buridan situations.

If Al were given the following instructions and chose to cooperate, his situation would be more similar to that of

Libet's subjects: Don't grab a jar of cashews without thinking. Instead, before you grab one, "note ... the time of appearance of [your] conscious awareness of wanting" to pick a particular jar, and be prepared to report that time after you pick a jar. Use the Libet wristwatch we just gave you to identify when this mental event happens.[11] It might occur to Al that should he become aware of wanting to grab jar $X$, he would have the option of acting on that want and the option of not acting on it. If he sees himself as having no reason to prefer either option to the other, he can pull a coin out of his pocket, arbitrarily assign heads to the former option and tails to the latter, and let what he does be settled by a coin toss—or he can save some time and effort by arbitrarily picking one of the options. Al's arbitrarily picking an option in this scenario can be described as "deciding on" that option. Someone who claims that Al is exercising free will in making his decision should point out that this is an instance of the liberty of indifference. Even if liberty or freedom of this kind is something to write home about, it is so only when one feels obliged to write and has nothing momentous to report. If free will were to come into play only when agents consciously select among options in Buridan situations, it would not be much more interesting than coin tosses that are used to break ties in such situations.

Al's feeling an urge to take jar $X$ puts him in a position to make a decision that he would have been in no position to make otherwise. Just as I cannot make a decision about whether to accept an offer of which I am not aware (for example, an offer to buy my house), Al cannot make a decision about whether to act on an urge of which he is not aware.[12] Given that he cannot make a decision about this, he cannot make a *free* decision about it. Awareness of particular options is important for deciding freely *among those options*. But this is not to say that one cannot freely decide to $A$ unless one first acquires an intention (or urge) to $A$—or an intention (or urge) not to $A$—and becomes aware of that intention (or urge). The awareness that I have highlighted as important is awareness of options to decide among, not awareness of intentions or urges to pursue those options— intentions or urges that one can then decide to veto or decide to act on. Some years ago, when I was deliberating about whether to accept an offer of the faculty position I now occupy, I weighed pros and cons and made a decision. I was well aware of my options. What did I decide? Did I decide to give the green light to my "conscious intention" to accept the job? No. At a time at which I am aware that I intend to *A* I cannot proceed to decide to *A*—that is, to form an intention to *A*. I cannot form an intention that I am aware I already have. Did I decide to veto my conscious intention to reject the offer. No, I never had such an intention. Nor, as far as I can tell, did I decide to give the green light to a conscious urge to accept the offer or decide to veto a conscious urge to reject the offer. Rather, what I decided to do was to accept the job offer. The decision I made was about that, not about conscious urges.

To the extent that Libet studies free will, he studies it in the sphere of proximal decision making in Buridan situations or situations of a similar kind. Generalizing from results obtained in this domain to a view about distal decisions made about important issues in situations of a very different kind would be extremely bold, to say the least. Even so, Libet is inclined to generalize: "our overall findings do suggest some fundamental characteristics of the simpler acts that may be applicable to all consciously intended acts and even to responsibility and free will" (1985, p. 563).

Within the sphere of the liberty of indifference, one sees oneself as having no reason for deciding to *A* rather than to *B* and vice versa. Given that fact, and given that decisions are caused, it is difficult to see why it should be thought that an agent not being conscious of the relatively prox- imal causes of his decisions in this sphere is interesting or important. Someone who assents to the following three propositions will conclude that we never decide freely: (1) the only possible location for free decisions is in the sphere of proximal decisions made in Buridan situations; (2) in such situations, both proximal decisions to *A* and proximal decisions to veto these decisions have their "origin[s] in preceding unconscious processes" (Libet 1999, p. 52); and (3) no decision that has its origin in preceding unconscious processes is free. Libet rejects proposition 2: he denies that the proximal decisions to veto at issue have unconscious origins. But whether proposition 2 is true or false is not of much consequence if proposition 1 is false. And Libet has given us no reason to believe that proposition 1 is true. (This is not the place to defend a position on the range of situations in which free decisions and other free actions are possible. On this issue, see Mele 2006.)

I turn to distal decisions. I have given more than a few talks on Libet's work; and more than once I have heard the suggestion that even if the objections I have raised to his claims about when proximal intentions to flex are acquired by his subjects are telling ones, Libet's work points to a serious worry about free will. The worry, it is said, is that we are not conscious of the relatively proximal causes of any of our decisions—including distal decisions—and, consequently, we never decide freely. Well, neural events are among the relatively proximal causes of our acts of deciding to *A*, and we are not conscious of those neural events as neural events. That we lack this consciousness should neither surprise nor worry anyone. The prospect that decisions have causes at all worries people who contend that (free) decisions must be uncaused. I have argued elsewhere against the possibility of uncaused decisions (Mele 2003, chap. 2) and for the possibility of decisions that are both free and caused (Mele 2006); and most of the philosophical views of free decisions currently in the running do not require that such decisions be uncaused. All free decisions are caused by events and states according to typical compatibilist views and event-causal libertarian views, and events and states are among the causes of all free decisions according to mixed or "integrated" agent-causal views.[13] Also, in situations in which we do decide an important issue one way or the other, we typically are aware of at least some of the considerations that influence us at the time (as I was in the case of the job offer I discussed).

Return to one of my acts of silently saying "now!" as a subject in a Libet-style experiment. I was unaware of the relatively proximal causes of that act. If someone had asked me why I said "now!" precisely when I did, rather than a bit earlier or a bit later in this Buridan situation, I would have reported that I had no idea. It certainly is not the case that I was aware of a proximal cause of that silent utterance and could cite it in answering the question. But we definitely should not infer from this—and facts like it about proximal decisions in similar Buridan situations—that I and other agents are never aware of any of the considerations that influence our decisions. If we never had any more insight into why we decided as we did than I did into why, at $t$, I proximally decided to flex (on the assumption that my silently saying "now!" at that time was an expression of a proximal decision to flex), we would be much more mysterious to ourselves than we actually are.

Libet asserts, as I have mentioned, that his "discovery that the brain unconsciously initiates the volitional process well before the person becomes aware of an intention or wish to act voluntarily . . . clearly has a profound impact on how we view the nature of free will" (2004, p. 201). If this "discovery" has had a profound impact on how some people view the nature of free will, that impact rests on error. That, in certain Buridan-like settings, potential relatively proximal causes of proximal intentions or decisions to $A$ arise unconsciously— events that may or may not be followed by an intention or decision to $A$—is a cause neither for worry nor for enthusiasm about free will.

NOTES

1. When does the *action* begin in all this—that is, the person's flexing his wrist or fingers? This is a conceptual question, of course: how one answers it depends on one's answer to the question "What is an action?" Libet identifies "the actual time of the voluntary motor act" with the time "indicated by EMG recorded from the appropriate muscle" (1985, p. 532). I favor an alternative position, but there is no need to disagree with Libet about this for my purposes here. Following Brand (1984), Frederick Adams and I have defended the thesis that overt intentional actions begin in the brain, just after the acquisition of a proximal intention; the action is proximally initiated by the acquisition of the intention (Adams and Mele 1992). (One virtue of this view is that it helps in handling certain problems about deviant causal chains: see Mele 2003, chapter 2.) The relevant intention may be understood, in Libet's words, as an intention "to act now" (1989, p. 183; 1999, p. 54; 2004, p. 148), a proximal intention. (Of course, for Libet, as for me, "now" need not mean "this millisecond.") If I form the intention now to start running now, the action that is my running may begin just after the intention is formed, even though the relevant muscular motions do not begin until milliseconds later.

2. Notice that in addition to "vetoing" urges for actions that are not yet in progress, agents can abort attempts, including attempts at relatively temporally short actions. When batting, baseball players often successfully halt the motion of their arms while a swing is in progress. Presumably, they acquire or form an intention to stop swinging while they are in the process of executing an intention to swing.

3. Two comments are in order here. First, those who view the connection as direct take the view that actions begin in the brain (see note 1). Second, Libet rejects the idea that conscious will is always involved in the triggering of

intentional actions (1999, p. 52); and I, of course, agree (see, e.g., my discussion of experienced drivers signaling for turns in chapter 2).

4. In this connection, see my discussion of Wegner's use of Libet's data in chapter 2.

5. One who deems a segment of what Libet calls the veto RP (1985, p. 538) to match averaged EEGs for type 300 activity may regard the matching as evidence that type 300 activity is not sufficient to produce (events that are sufficient for producing) a muscle burst around 0 ms.

6. I discuss a claim of this kind in chapter 6.

7. In a variant of this strategy, the clock hand getting very close to $p$ replaces the hand hitting $p$.

8. Brass and Haggard found some insula activation in inhibition trials, and they suggest that it "represents the affective-somatic consequences of failing to implement a strong intention" (2007, p. 9144). If this is right, subjects who display insula activation are not using strategy 2. Possibly, subjects who decide to *prepare* to press when the clock hand hits $p$ and then refrain from pressing would also display insula activation, in which case displaying such activation is compatible with using strategy 1. Strategies 3 and 4 both require the vetoing of decisions.

9. On determinism and deterministic causation, see chapter 8.

10. Ullmann-Margalit and Morgenbesser report that the example of the ass does not appear in Buridan's known writings (1977, p. 759).

11. The embedded quotation is from Libet, Gleason et al. (1983, p. 627).

12. Notice that my claim here does not entail that unconscious decisions are impossible. The claim leaves it open that we can make unconscious decisions about options of which we are aware. As always, by "decisions" here, I mean *practical* decisions—decisions about what to do.

13. In chapter 8, I cite compatibilist work by Harry Frankfurt, Michael Smith, and others. Robert Kane is a leading event-causal libertarian (see Kane 1996). Randolph Clarke (2003) develops an integrated agent-causal view. Readers unfamiliar with the terminology here will find guidance in chapter 8.

# FIVE

# Intentional Actions and The Alleged Illusion of Conscious Will

My primary task in this chapter is to ascertain whether the interesting phenomena that Daniel Wegner discusses in *The Illusion of Conscious Will* (2002) falsify a hypothesis about intentional actions that I formulated in chapter 1.

> *H*. Whenever human beings perform an overt intentional action, at least one of the following plays a causal role in its production: some intention of theirs; the acquisition or persistence of some intention of theirs; the physical correlate of one or more of the preceding items.

In chapter 2, to save space, I often suppressed the clause about physical correlates when discussing *H*. I do the same here. When I do not suppress reference to physical correlates, I use "intentions (or their physical correlates)" as shorthand for the long disjunction in *H*. When there is little risk of confusion, I sometimes use "intentions" as shorthand for that disjunction.

The truth of hypothesis *H* is not *required* for the existence of effective intentions, of course. If it were to turn out that there are effective intentions only in some cases of intentional action and that in others no item mentioned in *H* is at work, there would still be effective intentions. I focus on *H* in much of this chapter partly because so doing helps unify disparate data featured in Wegner (2002) and partly to set the stage for subsequent chapters.[1] The primary business of this chapter is completed in section 4. Section 5 takes up some recent claims by Wegner about free will and "the self."

## 1. Wegner on the Illusion of Conscious Will

In chapter 2, I reported Wegner's assertion that "conscious will is an illusion...in the sense that *the experience of consciously willing an action is not a direct indication that the conscious thought has caused the action*" (2002, p. 2). In itself, this assertion is not very informative. One wonders, for example, what "conscious thought" Wegner has in mind. Does he mean the conscious thought that one is willing an action? If so, exactly what is someone who thinks that he is willing an action supposed to be thinking? It is not as though the meaning of the sentence "I am willing an action"—or "I am willing this action of mine"—is transparent. That might help explain why I have never heard sentences like these in ordinary conversation.

As I mentioned in chapter 2, Wegner claims that "the experience of will is merely a feeling that occurs to a person" (2002, p. 14) and, more specifically, that "conscious will...is a feeling of doing" (p. 325). Accordingly, one may consider formulating the claim I quoted about illusion as follows: the feeling of doing "an action is not a direct indication that the conscious thought has caused the action." Again, what conscious thought?

Wegner's "new idea," again, "is the possibility that the experience of acting develops when the person infers that his or her own *thought* (read intention, but belief and desire are also important) was the cause of the action" (2002, p. 66). His instruction to read "intention" for "thought" provides an answer to my question in light of which the claim I quoted about illusion may be formulated as follows.

(*F1*) The feeling of doing "an action is not a direct indication
that the conscious [intention to perform the action] has caused
the action."

[In chapter 2, I noted that Anthony Marcel (2003) offers
what he regards as counterexamples to the idea that all intentions are conscious intentions.] Some of them feature distal
intentions. Because what is said in Wegner (2002) about
intentions primarily concerns proximal intentions, I set distal intentions aside in this chapter.[2] Attention to some of
Marcel's remaining attempted counterexamples will facilitate
discussion of Wegner's position. (As in previous chapters,
the default reading of "consciousness" is "report-level consciousness.")

Consider the following: "When I pick up something from
a low table I may be quite unaware whether I intend to do it
by bending at the waist or at the knee" (Marcel 2003, p. 60).
Wegner may reply that what the agent intends is to pick up
the object and that his intention does not extend to details
about bending. Alternatively, he may reply that even if the
agent has an intention that specifies these details, his thesis
about proximal intentions does not require that an idea of
*everything* that one is going to do intentionally at a time
appear in consciousness just before one does it. Thus, Wegner may say that even if Marcel intends to bend at the knee
when he picks up the object and intentionally bends at the
knee, Marcel's having the conscious idea of (intentionally)
picking up the object provides confirmation for Wegner's
thesis.

Marcel contends that "when I perform a subgoal *first* as a
discrete action, I may be unaware of intending it, for example, moving an object to get to the one behind it" (2003,
p. 60). Here, Wegner may try to benefit from a modest reading of "conscious intention" that I articulated in chapter 2.
He may claim that even if Marcel is not aware of his *intention*
to move the first object (as an intention), he may have been

conscious of an *idea* of moving it just before he moved it. Of course, this is not to say that Marcel would be persuaded by this maneuver. Perhaps Marcel would contend that he was not conscious of such an idea, and even so, he intended to move that object.

In chapter 2, I discussed Marcel's claim (2003, p. 61) that skilled tennis players sometimes run to the net with a proximal intention to put themselves in a position to hit, for example, a drive volley without being aware of it. Again, replies are available to Wegner. He can contend that the player becomes conscious of the idea of hitting the drive volley (maybe only faintly) as he is running to the net, despite the player's sincere denial of that,[3] or he can contend that if the player is not conscious of such an idea at the time, he lacks an intention to hit a drive volley. Again, Marcel might not be at all impressed.

In chapter 2, I motivated the thesis that given any of the interpretations offered there of "conscious proximal intention," including a very modest disjunctive one, not all proximal intentions are conscious intentions; and I offered a diagnosis of the disagreement between Marcel and Wegner. The diagnosis was this: whereas Marcel conceives of proximal intentions in terms of such functional roles as initiating, sustaining, and guiding intentional actions and does not take an agent's intentionally *A*-ing to require that he is conscious (aware) of *A*-ing, Wegner's conception of proximal intentions is motivated by his sensitivity to an apparent folk theory about or concept of such intentions according to which they are conscious products of conscious acts of will. Later, I explore some of the phenomena that Wegner discusses both on the hypothesis that nonconscious proximal intentions are conceptually possible and on the hypothesis that they are conceptually impossible.

Return to *F1*—the thesis that the feeling of doing "an action is not a direct indication that the conscious [intention to perform the action] has caused the action" (Wegner 2002,

p. 2). I prefer not to speculate about exactly what Wegner means by "direct indication." Instead, I consider the following, more precise, variant of *F1*.

> *F2.* An agent may have a conscious proximal intention to *A* and have a feeling of *A*-ing even if neither his proximal intention to *A* nor its physical correlate is a cause of his *A*-ing.

I follow Wegner in using "feeling" in such a way that someone who is not *A*-ing can have the feeling of *A*-ing. Accordingly, there are two potential routes to showing that *F2* is true.

> *Route 1.* One can try to find situations in which agents are not, in fact, *A*-ing even though they satisfy the following conditions: (*C*) they have a conscious proximal intention to *A* and have the feeling of *A*-ing.

> *Route 2.* One can try to find situations in which agents *A* while satisfying conditions *C* even though neither their proximal intentions to *A* nor the physical correlates of those intentions are causes of their *A*-ing.

A comment on the connection between Route 1 and *F2* is in order before I forge ahead. Readers who mistakenly read *F2* as entailing that the agent *A*-s will be confused about this connection. Notice that the truth of (*N*), "Neither *x* nor *y* is a cause of *S*'s *A*-ing," does not entail that *S A*-s. For any actual *x* and *y* that you pick, neither of them is a cause of Abraham Lincoln's climbing Mt. Everest. (For the record, Lincoln never climbed Mt. Everest. So, of course, nothing was a cause of his climbing it.) Just as *N* leaves it open whether the agent *A*-s, so does *F2*.

One who is looking for phenomena that confirm *F2* may also be looking more specifically for counterinstances to hypothesis *H* (reproduced in the opening paragraph of this chapter). Later, I discuss a way of using such phenomena in an effort to undermine *H* that is an alternative to the counterinstance strategy. I start with the strategy of searching for counterinstances.

Route 1 to showing that *F2* is true has at least two potential forms. In one, the person is not acting at all; in the other, he is acting but not *A*-ing. Now, because *H* applies only to cases of intentional action, situations in which the person is not acting at all cannot provide counterinstances to *H*. So suppose that an agent who satisfies conditions *C* is not *A*-ing and is doing something else instead—some overt intentional action, so that the episode has a chance of being a counterinstance to *H*.[4] This supposition is consistent with the agent performing an overt intentional action that has an item of one of the kinds specified in *H* as a cause.[5] That cause might even be an intention to *B*, if he is intentionally and overtly *B*-ing.

An illustration of this point is in order. Wegner discusses the practice of "facilitated communication," in which a "trained facilitator" holds the hand of "an impaired client...at a computer keyboard or letter board" (2002, p. 195). The clients are people with disorders that hamper speech, such as autism or cerebral palsy. Facilitators are supposed to help the clients express themselves without influencing which keys or letters the clients press or touch, and there is considerable evidence that this is what many of the facilitators intended to do and believed they were doing. "It was often [apparently] found that individuals who had never said a word in their lives were quickly able to communicate, typing out meaningful sentences and even lengthy reports" (Wegner 2002, p. 196). But it was also found that the clients' "responses actually originate with the facilitators themselves" (p. 197). Assume that some facilitators intended to facilitate communication without influencing the communication—that they intended to *FC*, for short. Assume, more specifically, that the following is true: some facilitators had conscious proximal intentions to *FC* in specific ways—for example, to *FC* now by moving a patient's hand in the direction they feel the patient wants to move it—and had the feeling of *FC*-ing in these ways, but because they were influencing the communication, they were not, in fact, *FC*-ing. The proposition just assumed entails *F2*. But it does not entail that *H* is false. The facilitators also had proximal intentions to hold clients' hands and to move their own arms in the direction they thought the clients were trying to move, and these intentions (or the acquisition of them, or relevant physical correlates, etc.) might have played a role in producing the facilitators' intentional arm and hand movements. (A facilitator may intentionally move his arm in a certain direction while unintentionally influencing his client's communication.)

These observations leave it open that a researcher *might* turn up, along Route 1, cases of intentional action that are counterinstances to *H*. My purpose in making them is to provide some guidance about what one should be looking for when trying to find counterinstances to *H*.

The second route I identified to showing that *F2* is true—Route 2—is to find cases in which agents *A* while satisfying conditions *C* even though neither their proximal intentions to *A* nor the physical correlates of those intentions are causes of their *A*-ing. Wegner's discussion of Libet's work has at least the appearance of direct relevance here. However, in chapter 2, I argued in effect that even if Wegner's suggestion that "conscious will" is "a loose end" in the process that generates the subjects' flexings (2002, p. 55) is correct, that would not undermine *H*. If, as Marcel and I maintain, agents can have nonconscious proximal intentions that produce corresponding intentional actions, an agent's conscious proximal intention to flex may produce a flexing action in a way that does not depend on the agent's consciousness of it. (Indeed, this may be true even if Marcel and I are wrong, as I explain in section 4.) Recall, in this connection, my observation in chapter 2 that the design of Libet's experiment may foster in subjects consciousness of proximal intentions to flex, that those intentions (or their physical correlates) may do their action-initiating work independently of the subjects' consciousness of them, and that they may do the same work when agents are not conscious of them. And notice again that *H* does not assign any role specifically to the agent's *consciousness* of intentions (nor to the physical correlates of such consciousness). This is just one illustration of a broader theme about intentions and consciousness. Others are forthcoming.

## 2. Hypothesis *H* and Table Turning

*H*, again, is the hypothesis that whenever human beings perform an overt intentional action, *A*, some intention of theirs, the acquisition or persistence of some intention of theirs, or the physical correlate of one or more of the preceding items plays a causal role in the production of *A*. In some cases, it may be unclear whether one should say that people are performing any overt intentional actions at all. Consider the phenomenon of table turning:

> A group of people sit gathered around a table, all with their hands on its surface. If they are convinced that the table might move as the result of spirit intervention...and sit patiently waiting for such movement, it is often found that the table *does* start to move.... Carpenter observed that "all this is done, not merely without the least consciousness on the part of the performers that they are exercising any force of their own, but for the most part under the full conviction that they are not." (Wegner 2002, p. 7)

Naturally, the people gathered at the table are moving it. But apparently, at least some of them are contributing to its motion without having any idea that this is so. Imagine that one of them, Tab, begins to feel some clockwise motion of the table. His hands move in the direction of the motion, as he notices, and he thinks he is merely allowing them to be dragged along by the table. In fact, however, he is pushing the table in that direction ever so slightly. Is Tab *intentionally* pushing the table along?

Probably, many people would say *no* and some *yes*. It is easy enough to talk someone out of a belief in the thesis that a person intentionally *A*-s only if he knowingly *A*-s. In an example I discussed in chapter 2, Al intentionally makes his daughter laugh with a funny e-mail message although he does not know that she is laughing and therefore does not know that he is making her laugh. But the story about table turning differs from Al's story in such a way that even someone who agrees both that intentionally *A*-ing does not entail knowingly *A*-ing and that Al intentionally makes his daughter laugh may consistently deny that Tab intentionally pushes the table along. Al knows that he is trying to make his daughter laugh, but Tab does not know that he is trying to push the table; that is a significant difference.

The truth of the claim that Tab does not know that he is trying to push the table is subject to two different diagnoses: (1) the claim is true because Tab is not trying to push the table (even though he is pushing it); (2) the claim is true because although Tab is trying to push the table, he does not know that he is. Just as people would disagree about whether it is correct to say that Tab intentionally pushes the table, they would disagree about whether it is correct to say that he tries to push the table (without realizing it). Not all people use the same words in the same way. Partly because Freudian theory has been absorbed into our culture, it should not be difficult to persuade people that agents can try to do things that they are not aware they are trying to do—for example, try to start a quarrel by complaining about a meal or try to hurt someone's feelings by making a joke that they consciously believe is inoffensive. (The same goes for intentions.) One way to try to bypass—at least temporarily—considerable quarreling about meaning in Tab's case is to ask whether, at the level of neural processes, Tab's pushing the table is caused in basically the same way that it would be caused if, say, he were consciously trying to push the table gently in a conscious attempt to trick others into believing that spirits are at work. (Readers who believe that, necessarily, one who is trying to *A* is consciously trying to *A* will read the preceding sentence as involving some redundancy.)

Wegner suggests that the answer to this question is *yes*: "Ideomotor action could occur by precisely the same kinds of processes that create intentional action.... Automatisms could flow from the same sources as voluntary action" (2002, p. 130). The following statement is much less tentative:

> Unconscious and inscrutable mechanisms create both conscious thought about action and the action, and also produce the sense of will we experience by perceiving the thought as cause of the action. So, while our thoughts may have deep, important, and unconscious causal connections to our actions, the experience of conscious will arises from a process that interprets these connections, not from the connections themselves. (Wegner 2002, p. 98)

Applied to the case of Tab, the idea, in part, is that the pushing is produced in the same basic way both in the actual and in the hypothetical scenario and that, in the latter scenario, because Tab knows what he is up to, he would have the experience of conscious will regarding his pushing of the table—the feeling of performing an action of table pushing.

Suppose that the answer Wegner suggests to my question about Tab is correct. This supposed truth may set the stage for the claim that Tab's pushing the table (without being aware that he is and without being aware of trying to do that) is a counterinstance to *H*, but it does so only if his

pushing the table counts as an *intentional* action. So suppose
that "intentional" is properly used broadly enough to include
Tab's unwitting table pushing. With that latter supposition in
place, it is not much of a stretch to the further supposition
that without being aware of it, Tab *intends* to push the table.
Might the physical correlate of this supposed intention have
a lot in common with that of the "conscious intention" to
push the table that Tab has in the hypothetical scenario in
which he is consciously trying to push the table? Consider
a conscious intention and subtract its consciousness aspect.
(Again, on the modest reading of Wegner's expression "conscious intention," this aspect is consciousness of "an idea of
what one is going to do.") What was subtracted and what
remains might each have its own physical correlate. If they
do, the physical correlates of Tab's "conscious intention" and
his nonconscious intention in the two scenarios may significantly overlap, the main difference being that in the hypothetical case something associated with the consciousness
aspect of Tab's intention is happening neurally that is not
happening in the actual case.

One can agree to count Tab's unwitting table pushing as an
intentional action and agree with Wegner that the pushing
is produced in the same basic way in both scenarios while
holding on to *H*. One can contend that in both scenarios
Tab has an intention to push the table that plays the same
basic role in producing a table pushing action or that in both
scenarios what is common to the physical correlates of the
"conscious intention" and the nonconscious intention plays
the same basic action-causing role. This is an indication that
Wegner's position is not nearly as radical as he seems to
think.[6] The expression "conscious intention" can mislead.
Saying that my conscious intention caused *x* leaves it open
what work (if any) was done by it being a *conscious* intention
(or the physical correlate of that feature of the intention)
in causing *x*. (Saying that Max struck the log with his red

ax, thereby causing the log to split, certainly does not entail that the redness of the ax did any work in causing the log to split.)

Wegner reports that his "analysis suggests that the real causal mechanisms underlying behavior are never present in consciousness" (2002, p. 97). As usual, he has the relatively proximal causes of behavior in mind. Again, in the case of many intentional actions, these causes may include proximal intentions of which the agent is not conscious (or the physical correlates of these intentions). The discussion in chapter 2 of experienced drivers signaling for routine turns dealt with an apparent case in point. Someone who conceives of intentions as essentially conscious will be blind to this point.

In my discussion of table turning thus far, I have focused on the question whether the phenomenon is a *counterinstance* to *H*. There is another way one might try to use the phenomenon in an attempt to undermine *H*. Consider the following argument.

1. Tab's pushing the table in the actual scenario is caused in basically the same way it would be caused in a hypothetical scenario in which he intentionally pushes the table in a conscious attempt to trick others.
2. Tab does not intend to push the table in the actual scenario.
3. So (from 2), neither an intention to push the table nor the physical correlate of such an intention is a cause of Tab's pushing the table in the actual scenario.
4. So (from 1 and 3), neither an intention to push the table nor the physical correlate of such an intention is a cause of Tab's pushing the table in the hypothetical scenario in which he intentionally pushes it in a conscious attempt to trick others.

The truth of a more fully stated version of 4 that also covers intention-acquisition, intention-persistence, and associated physical correlates would entail that *H* is false. Of course, the strength of the argument hinges on the strength of the evidence for premises 1 and 2. A proponent of this argument who does not distinguish between intending to *A* and consciously intending to *A* will defend 2 by marshaling evidence that Tab does not consciously intend to push the table. Someone who wishes to defend 1 should propose an account of how in both scenarios Tab's pushing the table is caused. Here, "ideomotor theory" enters the scene (Wegner 2002, p. 121).

Wegner writes: "With one sweep, [William] Carpenter proposed a central mechanism underlying table turning" and related phenomena.

> In essence, he said the idea of an action can make us perform the action, without any special influence of the will. This ideomotor action theory depended on the possibility that ideas of action could cause action but that this causal relation might not surface in the individual's experience of will. Thoughts of action that precede action could prompt the action without being intentions. (2002, p. 121)

Perhaps Carpenter's proposal provides a true account of how Tab's table turning is caused in the actual case, and perhaps his table turning is caused the same way in the hypothetical case, the central difference between the two cases having nothing to do with what actually causes the table turning actions. Perhaps. But if we are to be justified in rejecting *H*, we need more than a mere epistemic possibility. If nonconscious intentions are conceptually possible, it also is possible that some thought Tab had about the table in the actual case helped produce an intention to push the table that in turn helped produce his table turning action, even though he was not conscious of his intention and action. If the latter possibility is an actuality, premise 2 is false. It also is possible that Tab's table turnings in the two cases are not caused in basically the same way. If this possibility is an actuality, premise 1 is false. (I return to table turning in section 4.)

## 3. More on Ideomotor Action

Some additional phenomena that Wegner discusses under the rubric "ideomotor action" merit attention. I begin with "utilization behavior" (Lhermitte 1983, 1986). An examiner touches a brain-damaged patient's hands with an empty glass and a pitcher of water or a pack of cigarettes and a lighter (Wegner 2002, p. 122). "The frontal-damage patients may grasp the glass and pour it full from the carafe" or light a cigarette. "One patient given three pairs of eyeglasses donned them in sequence and ended up wearing all three." Wegner writes: "it is as though…the idea of the act that is suggested by the object is enough to instigate the action." However, a proponent of *H* would want to know whether we have good reason to believe that intentions to pour the water, light a cigarette, and put on glasses are not at work here. For example, does touching a patient's hands with a pack of cigarettes and a lighter make a causal contribution to his lighting a cigarette that is *not* indirect in the following way: the touching is a cause of the patient's acquiring an intention to light the cigarette, and his acquiring that intention is a cause of his lighting it? The observed phenomena do not provide a basis for an affirmative answer.

Consider some studies done in the late nineteenth century with an automatograph, a device consisting of "a piece of plate glass resting in a wooden frame, topped by three brass balls, upon which rested another glass plate" (Wegner 2002, p. 122). There also is a screen between the participant and a recording device that is attached to the automatograph. Wegner reports "some remarkable regularities" (p. 123). "Asked to count the clicks of a metronome…one person showed small hand movements to and fro in time with the rhythm."

Someone "asked to think of a building to his left...slowly moved his hand in that direction." A man who was invited to hide a knife in the room and then instructed to think about the object moved his hand in the direction of the knife "over the course of some 30 seconds."

These findings about "ideomotor action" can identify counterinstances to *H* only if the agents are performing overt intentional actions. My guess is that the great majority of people would say that the first agent does not intentionally move his hand to and fro, that the second does not intentionally move his hand to the left, and that the third does not intentionally move his hand in whatever direction he moves it—to the right, say. Even so, one can ask whether, at the level of neural processes, the hand movements are relatively proximally caused in basically the same way that they would be caused if these agents were consciously and intentionally moving their hands in these ways. If the correct answer is *yes*, perhaps the instructions these agents receive help generate intentions that play a role in producing the movements. (This is not to say, of course, that they are conscious of these intentions.) If the correct answer is *no*, one may try to use that fact in support of the claim that these hand movements are not intentional actions.

Of course, the counterinstance approach is not the only approach one can take in an attempt to undermine *H* with these findings about ideomotor action. In a passage that I quoted in part earlier, Wegner writes:

> Rather than needing a special theory to explain ideomotor action, we may only need to explain why ideomotor actions and automatisms have eluded the mechanism that produces the experience of will....Ideomotor action could occur by precisely the same kinds of processes that create intentional action but in such a way that the person's usual inference linking the thought and action in a causal unit is obstructed....Automatisms could flow from the same sources as voluntary action and yet have achieved renown

as oddities because each one has some special quirk that
makes it difficult to imbue with the illusion of conscious will.
(2002, p. 130)

One point I have made is that even if what Wegner here says
"may" and "could" be true actually is true, that is consistent
with one or another of the items featured in *H* playing a
role in the production of the actions at issue. For example,
if nonconscious intentions are possible, then because *A*-ing
does not entail having the feeling of *A*-ing, a nonconscious
intention can be at work in producing an action of which
the agent is unaware. I made another point in connection
with an alternative to the counterinstance strategy of under-
mining *H*. Although I made the point specifically about
table turning, it may be formulated more generally: even
if what Wegner says "could" be the case might be true, it
might also be false. For example, the hand movements in
the automatograph experiments might not be produced in
ways intentional actions are produced.[7] Wegner produces no
neurophysiological evidence that they are produced in the
same way.

## 4. Conscious and Nonconscious Proximal Intentions

I now call attention to two ways I have appealed to the conceptual possibility of nonconscious proximal intentions. The
first concerns Libet's subjects. In chapter 2, I observed that if
such intentions can be effective, then (*P1*) Libet's subjects'
conscious proximal intentions to flex (or their physical correlates) may produce flexing actions in a way that does not
depend on the subjects being conscious of those intentions
(nor on the physical correlates of that consciousness). I also
appealed to it in connection with my discussion of table
turning to illustrate the more general assertion (*P2*) that

saying that a conscious intention caused $x$ leaves it open what work (if any) was done by the agent's consciousness of the intention (or the physical correlate of that consciousness) in causing $x$. However, as I am about to explain, the conceptual possibility at issue is *not required* for the truth of *P1* or *P2*.

Suppose it is stipulated that it is conceptually *impossible* for an agent to have a nonconscious proximal intention. Some readers will view this stipulation as comparable to the stipulation that it is conceptually impossible for an object to be a pencil without being made partly of wood. We can agree to use the word "pencil" that way and call similar things made partly of plastic rather than wood something else. Similarly, we can agree to restrict our use of the word "intention" to conscious items of a certain kind. But even then, people who are inclined to think that "conscious intentions" are causes of intentional actions should wonder in virtue of what features proximal intentions (or their physical correlates)—and the acquisition and persistence of proximal intentions (or the physical correlates of these things)—play the various kinds of causal roles they may play and whether the consciousness that is built into the stipulated definition of "intention" (or the physical correlate of that consciousness) is at work in all of the causal roles played. Even if it is stipulated that necessarily all proximal intentions are conscious intentions, that leaves it open, for example, that different features of a particular proximal intention have different physical correlates and the physical correlate of the agent's consciousness of the intention is not at work in the production of some of the intentional actions produced by the intention (or by other parts of the intention's physical correlate).

I know of no good argument for the conceptual thesis that necessarily all proximal intentions are conscious intentions. My point in the preceding paragraph is that even theorists who assume this thesis to be true can consistently assent to *P1* and *P2*. And theorists who assent to these propositions are, other things equal, in a position to use one of the lines of argument I have used for the claim that the interesting phenomena Wegner (2002) discusses are consistent with the truth of hypothesis *H*. For example, it may be that Tab's pushing the table is caused in basically the same way that it would be caused if he were consciously trying to push the table gently, that his conscious intention is at work in the latter case, and that features of that conscious intention (or their physical correlates) other than the agent's consciousness of it (or the physical correlate of that consciousness) are doing the basic causal work. And as I have explained, if the table pushings are not produced in the same basic way and the unconscious table pushings are not intentional actions, the unusual phenomenon is not a problem for *H*.

Hypothesis *H* is still alive and well. I should note that in explaining how *H* can stand up against the phenomena Wegner discusses, I have not appealed to *distal* intentions that are directly relevant to some of the phenomena. For example, Libet's subjects presumably intend at the beginning of a session to flex many times over the course of the session.[8] Other things being equal, if they had not intended to do that, they would not have participated in the study. Following Wegner's lead, I focused on proximal intentions.

If the word "intentions" is treated as shorthand for the long disjunction in hypothesis *H*, then the truth of that hypothesis is compatible with the truth of each of the following propositions.

1. The only intentions that are among the causes of overt intentional actions are unconscious ones.
2. Some conscious intentions are among the causes of overt intentional actions, but the fact that an agent had a

   conscious intention to *A* never has a place in a causal
   explanation of a corresponding overt intentional action.
3. Some conscious intentions are among the causes of
   overt intentional actions, and sometimes the fact that an
   agent had a conscious intention to *A* has a place in a
   causal explanation of a corresponding overt intentional
   action.

My argument in this chapter that the phenomena discussed
in Wegner (2002) do not falsify *H* is not itself an argument
for 3. But it does help set the stage for an argument for 3.
In chapter 7, I discuss powerful evidence that 3 is true in
the case of some conscious distal intentions, and I discuss
a scenario in which 3 is likely to be true as well in the case of
some conscious proximal intentions.

I close this section by calling attention to a way that
some of the argumentation surrounding hypothesis *H* in
this chapter bears on 3. If unconscious intentions play a role
in the production of many actions, then, as I have mentioned, the instructions in some experiments—for example, many Libet-style experiments—may have the effect that
some subjects become conscious of intentions of which they
would otherwise have been unconscious. And it may be
that in some cases, the only interesting effect of a subject's
being conscious of the intention is his consciousness report;
the intention may issue in action independently of his consciousness of it. If that is how things are, then even if it could
be shown that in some Libet-style studies the fact that an
agent who *A*-ed had a conscious proximal intention to *A*
has no place in a causal explanation of his *A*-ing, it would
be a mistake to generalize from this finding to the claim
that the fact that agents had conscious intentions to *A never*
has a place in causal explanations of their *A*-ing. Obviously,
what is true of conscious proximal intentions that arise in a
peculiar setting might not be true of all conscious intentions.
I return to this issue in chapter 7.

## 5. Wegner on Free Will and the Magical Self

Wegner closely associates "conscious will" with free will. For example, in a précis of *The Illusion of Conscious Will*, he writes: "our discussion has actually been *about* the experience of free will, examining at length when people feel it and when they do not. The special idea we have been exploring is to explain the experience of free will in terms of deterministic or mechanistic processes" (2004b, p. 656).

In a discussion of Wegner's work, Daniel Dennett writes:

> If you are one of those who think that free will is only *really* free will if it springs from an immaterial soul that hovers happily in your brain, shooting arrows of decision into your motor cortex, then, given what *you* mean by free will, my view is that there is no free will at all. If, on the other hand, you think free will might be morally important without being supernatural, then my view is that free will is indeed real, but just not quite what you probably thought it was. (2003, p. 222)

Dennett adds that despite his admiration for Wegner's work, he sees Wegner as "the killjoy scientist who shows that Cupid doesn't shoot arrows and then insists on entitling his book *The Illusion of Romantic Love*" (2003, p. 224). One moral to take away from this is that if one sets the bar for free will—that is, for the power or ability to act freely—ridiculously high, the thesis that people sometimes act freely should strike one as ridiculous.  The moral is generalizable, of course: if one sets the bar for the existence or occurrence of *anything* ridiculously high, the assertion that it exists or occurs should strike one as ridiculous.

In Wegner's view, the illusion of conscious will is intimately related to a notion of "the self." He writes: "Each self is magic in its own mind" and "the magic self stands squarely in the way of the scientific understanding of the psychological, neural, and social origins of our behavior and thought" (2008, pp. 226–27). "Seeing one's own causal influence as supernatural is part of being human," Wegner asserts (2008, p. 228); and apparently, this vision is part of believing that one is (or has?) a self. If the bar for the existence or efficacy of "conscious will" is set so high that we have to be supernatural beings for conscious will to exist or be efficacious in us, then of course, conscious will should be lumped together with ghosts, fairies, and the like.

Wegner writes:

> Experience of apparent mental causation renders the self magical because it does not draw on all the evidence. We don't have access to the myriad neural, cognitive, dispositional, biological, or social causes that have contributed to the action—nor do we have access to the similar array of causes that underlie the production of the thoughts we have about the action. Instead, we look at the two items our magic selves render visible to us—our conscious thought and our conscious perception of our act—and believe that these are magically connected by our will. In making this link, we take a mental leap over the demonstrable power of the unconscious to guide action...and conclude that the conscious mind is the sole player. (2008, p. 234)

Obviously, even people who believe that some of their conscious intentions (or the physical correlates thereof) play a role in causing some of their behavior should not believe that "the conscious mind is the sole player." After all, among the things that play a role in causing our intentions are events in the external world. And if, for example, conscious proximal intentions play a role in causing overt actions, causal processes of which we are not conscious link them to bodily motions.

Wegner asks (2008, p. 228): "Why do we experience our actions as freely willed, arising mysteriously from the self, and why too do we resist attempts to explain those actions in terms of real causal sequences, events that are going on behind the curtain of our minds?" But why think of free will in terms of a magical self? Some alternative conceptions of free will are discussed in chapter 8.

How radical is Wegner's position? Such passages as the following may give the impression that it is very radical indeed:

> The magic of self...doesn't go away when you know how it works. It still feels as though you are doing things, freely willing them, no matter how much you study the mechanisms of your own behavior or gain psychological insight into how all people's behavior is caused. The illusion of self persists. (2008, pp. 236–37)
>
> I remain every bit as susceptible to the experience of conscious will as the next person. It feels like I'm doing things. (2008, p. 237)

It looks as though part of what Wegner is asserting here is that *we never do things*. That assertion—interpreted literally—is radical enough to grab the attention even of a philosopher who has heard arguments for skepticism about everything under the sun. If it were true, you would not be reading this sentence, for example; instead, you would have the illusion of reading it. But it is an excellent bet that by "you" and "I" in these passages Wegner means something like "your self" and "my self." It is true that our imaginary magical "selves" do not do anything. After all, they are only imaginary. But you and I exist, and we do lots of things. It is difficult to believe that Wegner would deny that.

Do we *freely* do things? That depends on how free action is to be understood. If (quoting Dennett again) "free will might be morally important without being supernatural," then maybe we sometimes act freely. If acting freely requires the existence of something that does not exist—a supernatural, magical self—then we never act freely.[9] But I know of no good reason to understand free action in the latter way. (On free action, see chapter 8.)

Exploring the extent to which the processes involved in the production of intentional actions are "automatic" and the extent to which they are "controlled" is an important and interesting project. In my opinion, the project can definitely stand on its own two feet. There is no need to motivate it by importing outlandish ideas to debunk: for example, the idea that supernatural, magical selves cause intentional actions. Motivating the project in that way is rather like motivating a study of human evolution by promising to prove that human beings were not created in their present form by God.

### NOTES

1.  Useful critical discussions of Wegner (2002) and related work of his are Bayne (2006), Holton (2004), Nahmias (2002), and many of the commentaries to which Wegner responds in Wegner (2004a). I review some of this work in Mele (2008c). Because my focus in this chapter is on *H*, I do not discuss Wegner's work on evidence that people can be caused to believe that they performed actions that they did not, in fact, perform. I review some of the literature on this issue in Mele (2008c).

2.  On distal intentions, see Wegner (2004a, p. 684).

3.  If Wegner were to take this position, he would be rejecting the idea (see chapter 2) that the correct measure of consciousness in scientific studies is subjects' reports.

4.  Recall my statement that Route 1 has *at least* two potential forms. What I identified as the second form is divisible into two forms. In one, although the agent is acting, he is not performing any *overt* intentional action; in the other, he is performing an overt intentional action.

5.  I remind readers who are not philosophers that as I use "consistent," to say that *p* is *consistent* with *q* is to say that "*p* and *q*" is not a contradiction.

6. Wegner writes: "Unfortunately, it has to be one way or the other. Either the automatisms are oddities against the general backdrop of conscious behavior causation in everyday life, or we must turn everything around quite radically and begin to think that behavior that occurs *with* a sense of will is somehow the odd case, an add-on to a more basic underlying system" (2002, p. 144).

7. Eddy Nahmias writes: "Another interpretation is that automatisms are *not* produced by the same kinds of processes that create intentional action precisely because the causal role of conscious intention has been bypassed" (2002, p. 533). Yet another is that some automatisms "are not produced by the same kinds of processes that create intentional action precisely because the causal role of ... intention"—conscious or otherwise—"has been bypassed."

8. Frederick Toates is making a similar point when he contends that although Libet's work "appears to cast doubt on the commonsense notion that we consciously form an intention and then later act as a result of it ... in agreeing to participate in Libet's study and perform a certain movement, the participants had already implemented a consciously accessible goal" (2006, p. 108). Toates cites Näätänen (1985) and Zhu (2003) in this connection.

9. Wegner certainly is not alone among scientists in understanding free will as something supernatural. After describing the threat that he believes Libet's work poses to free will, C. M. Fisher writes:

> Somewhat the same conclusion may be reached on the basis of rather elementary observation. Every thought, feeling, inclination, intention, desire ... must be created by nervous system activity. How else could they arise? Ideas would have to arise without a physical basis. Nervous system activity must always precede. ... If one has the experience of 'willing' the nervous system to do something, the impression of willing must have been preceded by nervous system activity. Otherwise there would be no source and we are in the realm of the supernatural. (2001, p. 56)

Mark Hallett offers a similar line of reasoning (2007, p. 1184) in partial support of the related thesis that "there does not appear to be a component process for producing voluntary movement that might be called 'free will' in the ordinary sense of the word" (p. 1189). He also contends that free will is nothing more than a misleading feeling or "perception" of "willing" a movement (pp. 1179–80, 1189).

• • •

# SIX

# Proximal Intentions and Awareness Reports

In chapters 3 and 4, I was willing to take the reports Benjamin Libet's subjects made about the time of their "initial awareness" of something that he variously describes as a decision, intention, urge, wanting, will, or wish to flex every bit as seriously as Libet does. I argued there that certain of Libet's striking claims are not warranted by his data, even if he is correct about the average time of initial awareness. However, there is a lively literature on how accurate subjects' reports of this time are likely to be (for a review, see van de Grind 2002), and some of the issues raised in it merit attention.

The following labels facilitate discussion of this chapter's primary topics.

*I-time*: The time of the onset of a proximal *intention* to *A* in a subject.

*C-time*: The time of the onset of the subject's *consciousness* or awareness of such an intention.

*B-time*: The time the subject *believes* to be *C*-time when responding to the experimenter's question about *C*-time.

How are these times related? Libet's position, again (see chapter 3), is that average *I*-time is −550 ms for subjects who are regularly encouraged to flex spontaneously and report no preplanning, average *C*-time is −150 ms, and average

$B$-time is −200 ms (1985, p. 532; 2004, pp. 123–26).[1] However, researchers who regard intentions as being essentially conscious (see chapter 2) identify $I$-time with $C$-time. Some who identify these times have suggested that $C$-time is too late to permit "motor intentions" to be among the causes of actions (Lau, Rogers, and Passingham 2007, p. 81). The issue about motor intentions and $I$-time is the topic of section 2. In section 1, I briefly describe a recent study that bears both on the issue of the accuracy of subjects' reports and on the connection between motor intentions and actions. I take up the issue of accuracy in section 3, along with the question of whether $C$-time is ever early enough for proximal intentions of which subjects are conscious to be among the causes of corresponding actions. Section 4 is a brief conclusion.

## 1. A Recent Study

A recent study by Lau, Rogers, and Passingham (2007) is motivated partly by Daniel Wegner's work on conscious will. Remarking on Libet's results (in a passage I discussed in chapter 2), Wegner writes: "The position of conscious will in the time line suggests perhaps that the experience of will is a link in a causal chain leading to action, but in fact it might not even be that. It might just be a loose end—one of those things, like the action, that is caused by prior brain and mental events" (2002, p. 55). Lau et al. observe that Wegner "does not show that motor intentions are in fact *not* causing the actions" and that "if intentions, in fact, arise after the actions, they could not, in principle, be causing the actions" (2007, p. 81). They proceed to discuss what they regard as evidence that in fact intentions do arise after associated actions.

The main experiment (Experiment 1) reported in Lau et al. (2007) combines Libet's clock paradigm with the application of transcranial magnetic stimulation (TMS) over the presupplementary motor area. The dot on their Libet clock revolves at 2,560 ms per cycle. While watching such a clock, subjects pressed a computer mouse button "at a random time point of their own choice" (p. 82). In the "intention condition," after a delay of a few seconds, subjects were required to move a cursor to where they believed the dot was "when they first felt their intention to press the button." In the "movement condition," they followed the same procedure to indicate where they believed the dot was "when they actually pressed the button." There were a total of 240 trials per subject. TMS was applied in half of the trials. Half of the applications occurred "immediately after action execution," and half occurred at a delay of 200 ms. There were 10 subjects.

Lau et al. discovered an effect that was not observed in a second experiment (Experiment 2) involving the application of TMS either at 500 ms after the button press or between 3,280 and 4,560 ms after it. "The effect observed in Experiment 1 [was] the exaggeration of the difference of the judgments for the onsets of intention and movement" (Lau et al. 2007, p. 87).[2] The mean of the time-of-felt-intention reports and the mean of the time-of-movement reports shifted in opposite directions from the baselines provided by the mean reports when TMS was not applied. The purpose of the second experiment, in which this effect was not found, was "to test whether the effect obtained in Experiment 1 was actually due to memory or responding, rather than the experienced onset itself" (p. 84).[3]

As Lau and his coauthors view matters, "the main question is about whether the experience of intention is fully determined before action execution" (2007, p. 87). Their answer is no: "The data suggest that the perceived onset of intention depends at least in part on neural activity that takes place after the execution of action" (p. 89).

## 2. Motor Intentions and Actions

Lau and coauthors take their results to bear on the question of whether motor intentions to press a mouse button, for example, are among the causes of the pressing actions. As I mentioned, they point out that Wegner has not shown that "motor intentions are in fact *not* causing the actions" and they observe that "if intentions arise after actions, they could not, in principle, be causing the actions" (2007, p. 81). Lau et al. seemingly believe that they have produced evidence that their subjects' proximal intentions to press arise after they press. But have they?

Return to the notions of $I$-time and $C$-time:

*I-time*: The time of the onset of a proximal intention to $A$ in a subject.

*C-time*: The time of the onset of the subject's consciousness or awareness of such an intention.

The time of the *onset* of $x$, for any $x$, is the time of $x$'s initial presence or of the occurrence of its earliest segment. Onsets of $x$ are, of course, to be distinguished from *causes* of onsets of $x$. Again, Libet identifies $I$-time with the time at which a type II RP begins, and he contends that average $I$-time precedes average $C$-time by over a third of a second. In chapter 3, I argued that Libet's position on this is unwarranted; but it should be noted that *if* the $I$-time for some intentions precedes the $C$-time for them, then *even if* the $C$-time is "after actions" (Lau et al. 2007, p. 81), the $I$-time might be early enough for the intention to play a role in causing the pertinent action. Lau et al. seem to assume, with Wegner (2002, p. 18), that nonconscious items cannot be intentions. However, as I explained in chapter 2, researchers who think of proximal intentions in terms of their functional roles tend to see no need for agents to be conscious of all of their proximal intentions.

Just as your nose is one thing and your awaren⟨
is another, might not a subject's proximal intention
a button be one thing and his awareness of that inte⟨
another? If so, two points need to be noted. First, the onset of
our awareness of some of our proximal intentions—in some
situations in which we are aware of them—may be significantly later than the onset of the intentions. Second, our
proximal intentions may play causal roles that our awareness
of them does not play.

Again, Lau et al. contend that "the data suggest that the
perceived onset of intention depends at least in part on
neural activity that takes place after the execution of action"
(2007, p. 89). But even if what they refer to as "the perceived
onset of intention"—that is, what the subjects *believe*, after
they press, about where the dot was "when they first felt
their intention to press" (p. 82)—depends partly on neural
activity that occurs after the subjects press, the data leave it
wide open that the *actual onset* of intention does not depend
on this neural activity and is early enough for the intention
to be among the causes of the action. Moreover, as I explain
in section 3, their data also leave it wide open that the time
of the onset of subjects' *consciousness* of proximal intentions
($C$-time) does not depend at all on "neural activity that
takes place after the execution of the action" (p. 89) and
that $C$-time is sometimes early enough for proximal intentions of which agents are *conscious* to play a role in causing
actions.

## 3. Accuracy

How accurate are subjects' reports about when they first
became aware of a proximal intention or urge likely to have
been? Framed in terms of $C$-time (the time of the onset
of the subject's consciousness or awareness of a proximal

intention to $A$) and $B$-time (the time the subject believes to be $C$-time when answering the experimenter's question about $C$-time), the question about intentions is this: how closely does $B$-time approximate $C$-time?

When, according to Lau and coauthors, do their subjects first become conscious of (or "perceive" or "feel") "their [proximal] intention to press the button" (2007, p. 82)? That is, what is $C$-time according to Lau et al.? In this connection, one should ask exactly what Lau et al. mean by their suggestion that "the perceived onset of intention depends at least in part on neural activity that takes place after the execution of action" (2007, p. 89). For example, do they mean to exclude the following hypothesis: the subjects are aware of a proximal intention before they press the button even though they do not have a definite opinion about when they perceived the onset of their intention—or when they first felt the intention (see note 2)—until after they act? Apparently not, for they grant that "it could be the case that some weaker form of experience of intention is sufficiently determined by neural activity that takes place before the execution of the action" (p. 89). I do not pretend to know exactly what Lau and coauthors mean by "weaker form" here. The point to be emphasized is that their results leave it open that subjects in the experiments at issue (sometimes or always) are aware or conscious of proximal intentions to press before they press and before they have a definite opinion about where the dot was on the clock when they first became aware of the intention. Lau and colleagues do not offer a definite answer about what average $C$-time is in their subjects; they are right not to do so, because the evidence they produce does not warrant such an answer. From the fact that $B$-time can be manipulated by TMS during or after an action, nothing follows about what average $C$-time is. And because this is so, the former fact also leaves it open that $C$-time is sometimes early enough for proximal intentions of which subjects are conscious to be among the causes of their actions.

There is a difference between becoming conscious of an intention and having an opinion about when one perceived the onset of one's intention. "Neural activity that takes place after the execution of action" (Lau et al. 2007, p. 89) may have an effect on one's *opinion about* when one first became conscious of one's intention even if it has no effect on when one *actually* became conscious of one's intention. For example, neural activity produced by TMS can have an effect on $B$-times without having an effect on $C$-times. Possibly, subjects' beliefs about when they first felt an intention to press the button are still in the process of being shaped 200 ms after they press; and this is compatible with their having become conscious of the intention before 0 ms. (Incidentally, even if the beliefs at issue are still in the process of being shaped at 200 ms, they may be in place by, say, 600 ms after the button press, and the window for TMS to effect $B$-time may be pretty small.) Experiments 1 and 2 cut little ice if what we want to know is when the subjects first became conscious of proximal intentions ($C$-time)—as opposed to when, after they act, they come to a definite opinion about when they first became conscious of these intentions and as opposed, as well, to how the time the subjects believe to be $C$-time when they make their reports ($B$-time) is influenced by neural processes that take place after action.

It may be that the beliefs that subjects report in response to the question about $C$-time are always products of their experience of a proximal intention (or decision or urge), their perception of the clock around the time of the experience just mentioned, and some subsequent events. Subjects may always estimate $C$-time based on various experiences rather than simply "remembering" it. And making the estimate is not a particularly easy task. Reading the position of a rapidly revolving dot at a given time is no mean feat, as Wim van de Grind observes (2002, p. 251). The same is true of relating the position of the dot to such an event as the onset of one's consciousness or awareness of a proximal intention to press a button.

Perhaps the difficulty of the task helps account for the considerable variability in $B$-times that individuals display across trials. Patrick Haggard and Martin Eimer (1999) provide some relevant data. For each of their eight subjects, they locate the median $B$-time and then calculate the mean of the premedian ("early") $B$-times and the mean of the postmedian ("late") $B$-times. At the low end of variability by this measure, one subject had mean early and late $B$-times of $-231$ ms and $-80$ ms, and another had means of $-542$ ms and $-351$ ms (p. 132). At the high end, one subject's figures were $-940$ ms and $-4$ ms, and another's were $-984$ ms and $-253$ ms. Bear in mind that these figures are for means, not extremes. These results do not inspire confidence that $B$-time closely approximates $C$-time. If we had good independent evidence that $C$-times—again, times of actual onsets of a subject's consciousness or awareness of a proximal intention—varied enormously across trials for the same subject, we might not find enormous variability in a subject's $B$-times worrisome in this connection. But we lack such evidence. Moreover, Lau et al. have produced evidence that $B$-times can be affected by neural activity that occurs "after the execution of a spontaneous action" (2007, p. 89); and, of course, no $C$-time that precedes "the execution of a spontaneous action" can be affected by anything that happens after the action. (Whether it ever—or always—happens that subjects become aware of a proximal intention to do something only after they do it is a legitimate question. But it is not answered by subjects' reports of $B$-times.)

One naturally wonders whether subjects who display relatively low variability in their $B$-times use different strategies for complying with the instructions than those who display relatively high variability. In future studies, asking subjects what they took their strategies to be might prove informative. Haggard notes that "the large number of biases inherent in cross-modal synchronization tasks means that the perceived time of a stimulus may differ dramatically from its actual onset time. There is every reason to believe that purely internal events, such as conscious intentions, are at least as subject to this bias as perceptions of external events" (2006, p. 82). Perhaps some subjects' strategies generate less bias than other subjects' strategies.

Is there a way to make the subjects' task a bit easier while also moving them a bit closer to something that might be regarded as simply remembering where the dot was at the onset of consciousness or awareness of some pertinent mental event? Consider the following instruction set:

> One way to think of deciding to press the button now is as consciously saying "now!" to yourself silently to command yourself to press the button at once. Consciously say "now!" silently to yourself whenever you feel like it and then immediately press the button. Look at the clock and try to determine as closely as possible where the dot is when you say "now!" Don't count on yourself simply to remember where the dot is then. Instead, actively make a mental note of where the dot is when you say "now!" and try to keep that note in mind. You'll report that location to us after you press the button.

$C$-time is not directly measured. Instead, subjects are asked to report, after they act, what they believe $C$-time was. This is a report of $B$-time. Is there a way of gathering evidence about which of various alternative sets of instructions might help yield $B$-times that are more reliable indicators of $C$-times? Some additional background sets the stage for an answer.

As Haggard observes, subjects' reports about their intentions "are easily mediated by cognitive strategies, by the subjects' understanding of the experimental situation, and by their folk psychological beliefs about intentions" (2006, p. 81). He also remarks that "the conscious experience of intending is quite thin and evasive" (2005, p. 291). Even if the latter claim is an overstatement and some conscious experiences of intending are robust, the claim may be true of many of the experiences at issue in Libet-style studies. One can well imagine subjects in Libet's or Lau et al.'s experiments wondering occasionally, for example, whether what they are experiencing is an urge to act or merely a thought about when to act or an anticipation of acting soon. Again, Lau and colleagues say that they require their subjects to move a cursor to where they believed the dot was "when they first felt their *intention* to press the button" (2007, p. 82; emphasis added). One should not be surprised if subjects given such an instruction occasionally wondered whether they were experiencing an intention to press or just an *urge* to press, for example. Subjects may also wonder occasionally whether they are actually feeling an intention to press or are mistakenly thinking that they feel such an intention. There is much less room for confusion and doubt about whether one is consciously saying "now!" to oneself. These observations generate a prediction: subjects asked to report on when they said "now!" will—individually—exhibit significantly less variability in their reports (relative to time 0) than those asked to report on onsets of awareness of such things as intentions and urges. If the prediction were shown to be true, we would have some grounds for believing that their reports about when they consciously said "now!" involve less guesswork and, accordingly, additional grounds for skepticism about the reliability of $B$-times in typical studies (that is, for skepticism about the hypothesis that $B$-times closely approximate $C$-times in these studies).

What about the "memory" part of the instruction set? It is difficult to predict what effect it would have. If the way people actually arrive at $B$-times is by estimating, after the fact, the pertinent position of the dot on the clock on the basis of various experiences, the memory instructions might be difficult to follow and result in greater variability.

Fortunately, there is a way to find out: namely, by running the experiment. One set of experiments can use the "now!"-saying instructions in place of the intention instructions, and another can combine the "now!"-saying instructions with the memory instructions, as described. It would be interesting to see how the results of versions of Lau et al.'s Experiments 1 and 2 that use instructions like these compare to the results they reported.[4]

I opened this section with the following question: how accurate are subjects' reports about when they first became conscious or aware of a proximal intention or urge likely to have been? *Not very* certainly seems to be a safe answer. But there may be ways to improve accuracy.

## 4. Conclusion

A summary of conclusions framed in terms of $I$-time, $C$-time, and $B$-time is in order.

> *I-time*: The time of the onset of a proximal intention to $A$ in a subject.
>
> *C-time*: The time of the onset of the subject's consciousness or awareness of such an intention.
>
> *B-time*: The time the subject believes to be $C$-time when responding to the experimenter's question about $C$-time.

Lau and coauthors provided evidence that subjects' $B$-times are influenced by the application of TMS at the time of a button press and 200 ms later. However this effect does not provide reliable information about what $I$-time is, nor about what $C$-time is. Consequently, their evidence about $B$-times does not support the thesis that proximal intentions always arise too late to be among the causes of actions nor the thesis that $C$-times are always too late for proximal intentions of which subjects are conscious to be among the causes of their actions. Lau et al. correctly assert that Wegner "does not show that motor intentions are in fact *not* causing the actions" (p. 81). They do not show this either—even regarding *conscious* proximal intentions. Even so, Lau et al.'s results are interesting. These results suggest that reports of $B$-times are reports of estimates that can be influenced by events that follow action. Further study of this issue may shed light on the issue of accuracy and on how long after action the onsets of the pertinent beliefs may be.[5]

Whether proximal intentions are ever among the causes of actions is a question that has attracted the attention of scientists and philosophers alike. The same is true of the question whether proximal intentions of which the agent is conscious are ever among the causes of actions. In future work of the sort reviewed here on these questions, researchers would do well to bear in mind the conceptual distinctions among $I$-time, $C$-time, and $B$-time. To the extent to which researchers wish to appeal to $B$-times in connection with either question, they should take steps to diminish the sources of inaccuracy. The same is true of researchers who wish to appeal to $B$-times in disputes about whether Libet was right or wrong in claiming that there is sufficient time to veto conscious proximal intentions (see chapter 4).

I close with a comment on Libet's work on free will. The following "discovery" is supposed to have "a profound impact on how we view the nature of free will" (Libet 2004, p. 201): in certain studies, the brain makes proximal decisions 550 ms before action begins (that is, at $-550$ ms), and the person becomes conscious of these decisions over a third of a second after they are made. In chapters 3 and 4, I showed (among other things) that it is improbable that what happens at $-550$ ms in these studies is that a proximal decision is made or a proximal intention acquired and that it is unknown how tightly connected what happens at $-550$ ms is to action; and in this chapter, I explained that there are good grounds for skepticism about the accuracy of the standard measure of the time of the onset of consciousness of a proximal intention. As I put it in chapter 4, Libet's discovery is not all it is cracked up to be.

## NOTES

1. Libet arrives at his average $C$-time of $-150$ ms by adding 50 ms to his average $B$-time ($-200$ ms) in an attempt to correct for what he believes to be a 50 ms negative bias in subjects' reports. For alleged evidence of the existence of the bias, see Libet (1985, pp. 534–35) and (2004, p. 128).

2. Actually, given that the subjects were asked to indicate where they believe the dot was "when they first felt their intention to press the button" (p. 82), what Lau et al. refer to as judgments about "onsets of intention" should be referred to as judgments about onsets of the feeling (or awareness) of intentions. Some readers may be curious about how the time of a key press is related to the time of the EMG activity that defines Libet's time 0. Haggard and Eimer report that EMG onset typically precedes key presses by 30 to 50 ms (1999, p. 130).

3. Lau et al. also report on two other experiments of theirs. They were designed to test whether the effect observed in the first experiment was "actually due to the general mechanism of cross-modal timing using the clock face" (p. 85) and whether it was due to "TMS noise added to the motor system" (p. 86).

4. EMG signals can be recorded from speech muscles even in silent speech (Cacioppo and Petty 1981; Jorgensen and Binsted 2005). Such recordings may be made in an experiment designed to compare what subjects subsequently report to be the time at which they silently said "now!" with the time of the onset of relevant EMG activity. Subjects' after-the-fact reports are (defeasible) evidence about when it was that they consciously silently said "now!" EMG recordings from, for example, the larynx in an experiment of the kind

at issue may be another form of (defeasible) evidence about this. A relatively simple experiment would leave overt action out. Subjects would be instructed to watch a Libet clock, consciously and silently say "now!" to themselves whenever they feel like it, and be prepared to report after the silent speech act on where the dot was on the clock when they said "now!" The times specified in the reports can be compared to the times of the onset of relevant EMG activity.

5. As I mentioned, in Experiment 1 TMS was applied at a delay of either (1) 0 ms or (2) 200 ms, and in Experiment 2 it was applied at a delay of either (3) 500 ms or (4) between 3,280 and 4,560 ms. The group means for the TMS effects in the intention condition were as follows for these delays: (1) −9 ms, (2) −16 ms, (3) 9 ms, (4) 0 ms. This may suggest that subjects' beliefs about when they first felt their intention are still in the process of being formed at delay time 2 and are in place before delay time 4. The finding that "the effect observed in Experiment 1, that is, the exaggeration of the difference of the judgments for the onsets of intention and movement," was not observed in Experiment 2 (Lau et al. 2007, p. 87) is less directly relevant to this suggestion. The effect reported in the passage just quoted is a statistically stronger effect than the TMS effect in the intention condition alone in Experiment 1. That is why Lau and colleagues focus on it even though the movement judgments and the effects of TMS on them tell us little about $I$-time, $C$-time, or $B$-time.

• • •

# SEVEN

# The Power of Conscious Will

As I observed in chapter 5, saying that my conscious intention or decision caused $x$ leaves it open what work (if any) is done by its being a *conscious* decision or intention (or by the physical correlate of that feature of the decision or intention) in causing $x$. (Hereafter in this chapter, I suppress reference to physical correlates.) Might the fact that an agent *consciously* makes a proximal decision to press a button in a Libet-style experiment ever have a place in a causal explanation of a button press? Might similar facts about some conscious distal decisions or intentions similarly have a place in causal explanations of corresponding overt actions? These questions—especially the second one—guide this chapter.

## 1. Proximal Decisions and an Imaginary Experiment

Imagine a study in which subjects are instructed to make conscious decisions to press and then press straightaway in response to those decisions. It is made very clear to them that they are not to press unless they first consciously make a proximal decision to press. Suppose that Sam, a subject in this hypothetical experiment, succeeds in following the instructions—literally interpreted—on a particular occasion. At time $t$, he makes a conscious proximal decision to press the button and he proceeds to execute that decision.

Consider the following two claims:

*C1.* If, at $t$, Sam had not consciously made a proximal decision to press, he would have pressed at the same time anyway, owing perhaps to an unconscious proximal decision or intention to press.

*C2.* If, at $t$, Sam had not consciously made a proximal decision to press, he would not have pressed the button when he did; instead, he would have consciously made a decision of this kind a bit later, and he would have executed that decision.

If we assume that Sam is good at following his instructions, we should view *C2* as much more plausible than *C1*. *C2* supports the following claim:

*C3.* The fact that, at $t$, Sam *consciously* made a proximal decision to press the button helps account for the fact that he pressed the button at $t + n$.

A critic may make the following claim about the proximal decision that Sam made at $t$: even if that decision had not been a conscious decision, it would have done the work that proximal decisions do; accordingly, it would have issued in Sam's pressing the button at $t + n$. Someone who makes this claim may infer that even if Sam is good at following his instructions, *C3* is false.

The inference is misguided. Even if an unconscious proximal decision to press would have been just as effective as a conscious one, it is very likely that if Sam had not *consciously* proximally decided at $t$ to press the button, he would not have proximally decided at $t$ to press the button and would not have pressed it at $t + n$. (Again, given that he is good at following his instructions, it is likely that Sam would instead have consciously decided a bit later to press the button and would have pressed it later than $t + n$.) This supports *C3*.

Consider an analogy. Max struck a log with his red ax, thereby causing the log to split. If Max's ax had been green, it would have split the log just as well. But he was under strict instructions to split wood only with red axes, and he was committed to following the instructions. If his ax had been green, he would not have used it; in fact, he would have looked for a red ax and split the log later, after he found one. In this scenario, the fact that the ax is red is causally relevant to Max's splitting the log *when* he does and therefore to the actual log splitting action he performed, an action that has a specific location in time. Similarly, in the imagined experiment, the fact that at *t*, Sam made a *conscious* proximal decision to press seems to be causally relevant to his pressing when he does and therefore to the actual pressing action he performs. I should add that although we do know that, other things equal, red and green axes split wood equally well, we do not know how effective unconscious decisions are. Nor do we know whether unconscious deciding (as distinct from unconscious nonactional intention acquisition) is something that actually happens. Also, for all we know, if there are instances of unconscious deciding, they are far too rare for there to be more than a glimmer of a chance that if Sam had not made a conscious proximal decision to press at *t*, he would have made an unconscious one.

The instructions in the imaginary experiment that I have been discussing are no more peculiar than the instructions in Libet's main study. But they are different. The imaginary instructions encourage subjects to be active in a specific way that Libet's instructions do not. They encourage subjects specifically to make proximal *decisions* to press—that is, actively to form proximal intentions to press.

Despite this feature of the imaginary instructions, it would be difficult to be certain that subjects are actually making such decisions. To see why, consider another imaginary experiment in which subjects are instructed to count—consciously and silently—from one to five and to press just after they consciously say "five" to themselves. Presumably, these instructions would be no less effective at eliciting pressings than the "conscious decision" instructions. In this experiment, the subjects are treating a conscious event—the conscious "five"-saying—as a "go" signal. (When they say "five," they are not at all uncertain about what to do, and they make no *decision* then to press.) Possibly, in a study in which subjects are given the "conscious decision" instructions, they would not actually make proximal decisions to press but would instead consciously simulate deciding and use the conscious simulation event as a "go" signal.

Ascertaining whether the fact that an agent consciously makes a proximal decision to A ever has a place in a causal explanation of his A-ing is a difficult task. Among other things, to be confident that data about the output end of things (for example, about the onset of muscle activity) are relevant, we would need to be confident that the agents are actually deciding to A, as opposed, for example, to using some other kind of conscious event as a "go" signal. Is this a problem only for those who would like to believe in the efficacy of conscious proximal decisions? Definitely not. It is also a problem for those who claim to have shown with Libet-style studies that the fact that an agent consciously makes a proximal decision to perform an overt action never has a place in a causal explanation of such an action.

## 2. Implementation Intentions: Some Findings

I turn from my imaginary study to actual studies. Do any controlled studies yield evidence that the fact that an agent consciously decided to A or had a conscious intention to A sometimes has a place in a causal explanation of a corresponding overt intentional action? Following the lead of such scientists as Libet and Wegner, I have been focusing on *proximal* decisions and intentions in this book, but I would be remiss to ignore work on distal "implementation intentions" in the present connection (Gollwitzer 1993, 1996, 1999; Gollwitzer and Sheeran 2006). Implementation intentions, as Peter Gollwitzer conceives of them, "are sub-ordinate to goal intentions and specify the when, where, and how of responses leading to goal attainment" (1999, p. 494). They "serve the purpose of promoting the attainment of the goal specified in the goal intention." In forming an implementation intention, "the person commits himself or herself to respond to a certain situation in a certain manner."[1]

In one study of subjects "who had reported strong goal intentions to perform a BSE [breast self-examination] during the next month, 100% did so if they had been induced to form additional implementation intentions" (Gollwitzer 1999, p. 496). In a control group of people who also reported strong goal intentions to do this but were not induced to form implementation intentions, only 53 percent performed a BSE. Subjects in the former group were asked to state in writing where and when they would perform a BSE during the next month. The intentions they consciously expressed in writing are implementation intentions. If, in response to the request, these subjects actively formed relevant implementation intentions, they *decided* in advance on a place and time for a BSE.

Another study featured the task of "vigorous exercise for 20 minutes during the next week" (Gollwitzer 1999, p. 496). "A motivational intervention that focused on increasing self-efficacy to exercise, the perceived severity of and vulnerability to coronary heart disease, and the expectation that exercise will reduce the risk of coronary heart disease raised compliance from 29% to only 39%." When this intervention was paired with the instruction to form relevant implementation intentions, "the compliance rate rose to 91%."

In a third study reviewed in Gollwitzer (1999), drug addicts who showed symptoms of withdrawal were divided into two groups. "One group was asked in the morning to form the goal intention to write a short curriculum vitae before 5:00 p.m. and to add implementation intentions that specified when and where they would write it" (p. 496). The

other subjects were asked "to form the same goal intention but with irrelevant implementation intentions (i.e.,
they were asked to specify when they would eat lunch and
where they would sit)." Once again, the results are striking:
although none of the participants in the second group completed the task, 80 percent of the subjects in the first group
completed it.

Many studies of this kind are reviewed in Gollwitzer
(1999), and Gollwitzer and Sheeran report that "findings
from 94 independent tests showed that implementation
intentions had a positive effect of medium-to-large mag-
nitude...on goal attainment" (2006, p. 69). Collectively,
the results provide evidence that the presence of relevant
distal implementation intentions significantly increases the
probability that agents will execute associated distal "goal
intentions" in a broad range of circumstances. In the experimental studies that Gollwitzer reviews, subjects are explic-
itly asked to form relevant implementation intentions, and
the intentions at issue are consciously expressed (1999,
p. 501).

It should not be assumed, incidentally, that all members
of all the control groups lack conscious implementation
intentions. Indeed, for all anyone knows, most members of
the control groups who executed their goal intentions consciously made relevant distal implementation decisions.

## 3. Implementation Intentions
## and Decisions: Causal Issues

What should be made of the data discussed in the preceding section? An *illusion theorist* about conscious decisions
and intentions claims that such decisions and intentions are
never, in fact, among the causes of corresponding actions.
In light of the data on implementation intentions, is this a
plausible position to take?

Return to the BSE study, in which the success rate was 100 percent for the implementation-intention group (group 1) and 53 percent for the control group (group 2). Consider the following pair of claims:

*C4.* If the subjects in group 1 had not been asked to form and report relevant distal implementation intentions, they would have had a 100 percent success rate anyway, owing partly perhaps to distal implementation intentions of which they were not conscious.

*C5.* If the subjects in group 1 had not been asked to form and report relevant distal implementation intentions, they would have had a success rate much closer to 53 percent than to 100 percent.

Obviously *C5* is much more plausible than *C4*. The only basic difference between groups 1 and 2 that is known to be relevant is the difference in instructions, and that difference is associated with a 100 percent versus a 53 percent success rate. If the subjects in group 1 had not been asked to form and report relevant distal implementation intentions, their circumstances would have been just the same as those of the subjects in group 2, and they would probably have had a success rate very similar to that of group 2. Someone might contend that, even so, it is not the *having* of conscious distal implementation intentions that accounts for the impressive success rate of group 1 but, instead, the sincere *reporting* of distal implementation intentions. This contention is testable. Another group of subjects reporting strong goal intentions to perform a BSE during the next month may be asked to decide during the experiment—consciously, of course—where and when they will perform it without also being asked to report their decision. I would not be surprised if it were discovered that although the reporting has some effect, it is not nearly great enough to account for the difference between groups 1 and 2. When tests are conducted, there will be no need to speculate about this.[2]

An illusion theorist about conscious intentions may claim (1) that distal implementation intentions of which the agents were never conscious would have been just as effective as the subjects' conscious distal implementation intentions, and (2) that the fact that these intentions are conscious intentions therefore is causally irrelevant to the performance of BSEs.[3] Claim 1 is extremely bold, to say the least. How would the imagined unconscious distal intentions help generate corresponding actions days or weeks later? Seemingly, not as a consequence of agents consciously remembering these intentions when the time for their execution is near. Proponents of claim 1 should specify a process that links distal implementation intentions of which agents are never conscious to corresponding intentional actions and produce evidence that the specified process is not a fiction. Once that is done, they can turn their attention to supporting their assertion of equal effectiveness.

Even if claim 1 were granted, that would not settle matters. If 1 is true, then what accounts for the different success rates in the two groups? Apparently, that many people in group 2 do not acquire relevant implementation intentions. One way for subjects to acquire distal implementation intentions is to do so consciously but nonactionally as the upshot of conscious reflection on when and where to perform a BSE. Their conscious reflection may issue, for example, in a conscious belief that it would be best to perform a BSE at a certain place and time, and in the absence of an act of *deciding*, that belief may issue in a conscious distal implementation intention. Another way to acquire relevant implementation intentions is to consciously *decide* in advance (after some conscious reflection) to perform a BSE at a certain place and time. If the distal intention formed in that conscious act of deciding plays a causal role in the production of the action, the conscious decision is in the causal chain.

To say that the conscious decision is in the causal chain is not yet to say that the fact that it is a *conscious* decision has a place in a causal explanation of a corresponding overt action. An illusion theorist may claim that unconscious distal implementation decisions would have been just as effective as conscious ones in producing BSEs. As in the case of the claim (1 above) that distal implementation *intentions* of which the agents were never conscious would have been just as effective as the subjects' conscious distal implementation intentions, granting the present claim would not settle matters.

Three observations collectively help explain why. First, even if unconscious implementation decisions and intentions are just as effective as conscious ones—and this, of course, is disputable—this does not entail that the fact that an agent made a conscious distal implementation decision about a BSE has no place in a causal explanation of her execution of a related goal intention. Consider an analogy. Sally's mother driving her to school and Sally's father driving her to school are equally effective ways of bringing it about that Sally arrives at school. But that obviously does not entail that the fact that Sally's mother drove her to school today has no place in a causal explanation of Sally's arriving at school today. Now, consciously deciding in advance to conduct a BSE at a certain place and time is a way of acquiring an implementation intention to do that. If unconsciously deciding in advance to do this is possible, then that is another way of acquiring a relevant implementation intention. Just as the fact that Sally's mother drove her to school today has a genuine place in a causal explanation of Sally's arriving at school today, so may the fact that a subject consciously made a certain implementation decision have a genuine place in a causal explanation of her conducting the BSE. More precisely, the supposed fact that an unconscious implementation decision would have been just as effective does not preclude this.

I set the stage for my second observation with a reminder. Recall that in my hypothetical experiment with Sam (in section 1), it is very likely that if at *t* he had not consciously made a proximal decision to press, he would not have pressed the button when he did. Similarly, in the BSE scenario, the following counterfactual is very plausible.

> *CD*. If an agent who consciously decided in advance to perform a BSE at a place $p$ and a time $t$ and later executed that decision had not consciously decided to do that, she would not have performed a BSE at that place and time.

There is no reason to believe that if she had not consciously decided to do that, she would have unconsciously decided on the same place and time or nonactionally acquired an unconscious implementation intention specifying that very place and time. And, of course, even if an unconscious implementation intention specifying that place and time were to emerge, we would still want an answer to a question I raised earlier—how is the intention supposed to help generate a corresponding action at that later place and time? The likely truth of *CD* supports the claim that the fact that the agent consciously decided to perform a BSE at $p$ and $t$ has a place in a causal explanation of the corresponding overt action—an action occurring at a specific place and time.

A critic may contend that *CD* is irrelevant for present purposes and that the following counterfactual *is* relevant.

> *CD\**. If an agent who consciously decided in advance to perform a BSE at a place $p$ and a time $t$ and later executed that decision had not consciously decided to do that and instead had unconsciously decided to do that, she would have performed a BSE at that place and time.

The critic may contend that *CD\** is true and that its truth entails that the fact that the agent consciously decided to perform a BSE at $p$ and $t$ is causally irrelevant to her performing it there and then. Now even if unconscious distal implementation decisions are not only possible but actual, we have no idea how effective they tend to be. So confidence that *CD\** is true is definitely unwarranted. And even if *CD\**

is true, the critic's claim about entailment is false. For if that claim were true, the truth of the following counterfactual would entail that the fact that Sally's mother drove her to school today is causally irrelevant to Sally's arriving at school today: (*TD*) if Sally's mother had not driven her to school today, and instead her father had driven her to school, Sally would have arrived at school today.

I introduce the final member of my trio of observations with a question I asked about the BSE study. If unconscious implementation decisions and intentions are just as effective as conscious ones, why do the subjects in group 1—all of whom have conscious implementation intentions to perform BSEs at particular places and times—do so much better than those in group 2? Apparently, because not nearly as many members of group 2 have relevant implementation intentions, conscious or otherwise. Given the illusionist suppositions in play about unconscious implementation decisions and intentions—namely, that they exist and are just as effective as conscious ones—it is clear that in the studies under consideration, people are much more likely to have conscious implementation intentions than unconscious ones. Given the illusionist suppositions, we have no grounds for believing that if people who consciously decide in advance to *A* at a certain place and time were not to make such conscious decisions, all of them would make relevant unconscious implementation decisions or acquire relevant implementation intentions in some other way. Instead, there is evidence that if unconscious distal implementation decisions and intentions are just as effective as conscious ones, some people who make conscious implementation decisions and execute their corresponding goal intentions would lack implementation intentions in the absence of such a conscious decision and would not execute their goal intentions. And the consequent of the preceding conditional supports the claim that the fact that some people make conscious implementation decisions is causally relevant to the corresponding actions they perform. Finally, if unconscious distal implementation decisions and intentions are *less* effective than conscious ones, then—obviously—conscious ones are *more* effective. Presumably, what would account for that difference is some other difference between conscious and unconscious implementation decisions and intentions—bad news for illusionists!

You and I make many conscious implementation decisions, even if no experimenters invite us to do so. We do so when we plan complicated trips, parties, conferences, and the like. The argumentation in the preceding paragraph that is not specifically about controlled studies applies to the full range of conscious implementation decisions, not just those evoked by experimenters.

Regarding studies of implementation intentions, the bottom line is that if subjects sometimes make conscious implementation decisions, we have good reason to believe that the fact that they are *conscious* decisions is causally relevant to their corresponding overt actions. This is not surprising. Perhaps some readers were not aware of studies like Gollwitzer's before they read this section. It might have struck some such readers that their success rate at executing distal "goal intentions" would improve significantly if they were to have suitable distal implementation intentions more often than they ordinarily do. If some readers find an improvement of this kind desirable, what should they do? Should they sit back and hope that useful unconscious distal implementation intentions will emerge in them? Would it be better consciously to settle on a policy of trying to bring it about that they have relevant implementation intentions on suitable occasions; consciously to think, when such occasions arise, about where and when to execute their goal intentions; and consciously to decide on a place and time in situations in which their conscious reflection about where and when to act leaves the matter unsettled? The answer is obvious.

As I observed in chapter 2, in some scenarios, instructions may render subjects aware of proximal intentions to do things that they would otherwise have had unconscious proximal intentions to do. Recall the discussion of experienced drivers who are instructed to report after flipping a turn indicator when they first became aware of an intention to flip it. Their being conscious of these intentions enables them to report on the intentions, but it should not be expected to result in marked improvement of their turn-signaling behavior. In the studies of distal implementation intentions that Gollwitzer reviews, matters are very different. Either the instructions—which prompt *conscious* implementation intentions—significantly increase the probability that the subjects will have distal implementation intentions or distal implementation intentions of which agents are never conscious generally are not nearly as effective as conscious ones; and the presence of conscious distal implementation decisions and intentions is correlated with markedly better performance.

I should emphasize that the "or" in the preceding sentence is inclusive. The instructions in the experiments at issue certainly seem to increase the probability that subjects will have distal implementation intentions—in particular, conscious ones that are, on the whole, remarkably effective. And we have no grounds for confidence that distal implementation intentions of which agents are never conscious are as effective as consciously formed or acquired ones. In fact, even finding evidence of the existence of unconscious intentions of this kind in human beings—not to mention evidence of the existence of processes that link such intentions to corresponding actions of ours days or weeks later—is no mean feat. The conscious formation or acquisition of distal implementation intentions promotes conscious memory, at appropriate times, of agents' intentions to perform the pertinent actions at specific places and times, which increases the probability of appropriate intentional actions. How do distal implementation intentions and decisions of which we are never conscious do their alleged work in us? Answering this question is left as an exercise for the reader. If and when ambitious readers produce evidence that we have such intentions and make such decisions, they can get to work on finding evidence about processes that link the intentions and decisions to corresponding actions days or weeks later, and they can investigate the reliability of these processes.

There is powerful evidence for the truth of the following thesis: the fact that an agent consciously decided to *A* or had a conscious intention to *A* sometimes has a place in a causal explanation of a corresponding overt intentional action. Illusion theorists reject this thesis. Things look very bleak for them.

## NOTES

1. Although a proximal intention can "specify the when, where, and how" (Gollwitzer 1999, p. 494) of a response leading to the attainment of a goal one already has, the implementation intentions that concern Gollwitzer are distal intentions.

2. I suggested a study of the kind just sketched to Peter Gollwitzer, who said he would arrange to have it conducted. The results should prove instructive.

3. Of course, Wegner is in no position to make claim 1, given his view that intentions are essentially conscious (see chapter 2).

• • •

# EIGHT

# Conclusion

In chapters 3 and 4, I argued that Benjamin Libet's provocative claims about decisions, intentions, and free will are not warranted by his data. In chapter 5, I argued that the interesting phenomena that Daniel Wegner discusses in defending his illusion thesis about conscious will are consistent with the truth of the hypothesis ($H$) that whenever human beings perform an overt intentional action, at least one of the following plays a causal role in its production: some intention of theirs, the acquisition or persistence of some intention of theirs, or the physical correlate of one or more of the preceding items. In chapter 6, I argued, among other things, that Hakwan Lau and his coauthors have not shown that conscious proximal intentions always emerge too late to be among the causes of corresponding intentional actions. In chapter 7, I argued that there is powerful empirical support for the claim that the fact that an agent consciously decided to $A$ sometimes has a place in a causal explanation of an intentional $A$-ing. I definitely have not argued that Libet's, Wegner's, and Lau's theses are in principle unsupportable, *necessarily* false, or anything of the sort. Rather, my tack was to argue that the *data* to which they appeal do not warrant certain bold conclusions.

After talks I have given on scientific work on intentional human action or free will, I have sometimes been asked what kinds of hypothetical empirical discovery would persuade me of such things as that Wegner's "epiphenomenalism" about proximal intentions is true, that hypothesis $H$ is false, that all proximal intentions are acquired unconsciously, or that no one has free will. That is a fair question. Attention to it will reinforce some points I have made and give me the opportunity to make some observations about free will that readers who are not well acquainted with the philosophical literature on the topic should find useful. The question about hypothetical empirical discoveries is the topic of sections 1 and 2. Section 3 wraps things up.

## 1. Epiphenomenalism, Proximal Intentions, and Hypothetical Empirical Discoveries

If the expression "proximal intentions*" is used as a label for a collection composed of proximal intentions, their acquisition, and their persistence, then what I dub *philosophical epiphenomenalism* about proximal intentions* is the thesis that although all proximal intentions* are caused by physical events, no proximal intentions* cause any physical events. Hypothesis $H$ does not contradict philosophical epiphenomenalism about proximal intentions*. One can coherently contend that even though $H$ is true, the physical correlates of proximal intentions* cause physical events, and proximal intentions* themselves, though they are caused by physical events, never cause any physical events (e.g., any of the physical events involved in my typing this sentence). However, this coherent contention depends for its truth on metaphysical truths. From a physicalist neuroscientific point of view, proof that the physical correlates of proximal intentions* cause physical events constitutes proof that proximal intentions* cause physical events. It is primarily philosophers who would worry about the metaphysical intricacies of the mind–body problem despite accepting the imagined proof about physical correlates, and the relevant argumentation would be distinctly philosophical.[1] Wegner's own "epiphenomenalism" about proximal intentions extends to the physical correlates of such intentions (as *he* understands intentions); and his claim is not that proximal intentions (as he understands them) and their physical correlates cause no physical events at all (see 2002, pp. 325–28), but that they do not cause any of the physical events that intentions are thought by many people to cause—events involved in corresponding overt intentional actions.

Wegner's epiphenomenalism is not philosophical epiphenomenalism. Hypothetical empirical discoveries that would convince me that hypothesis $H$ is false would convince me that something entailed by his epiphenomenalism is true, if his epiphenomenalism entails the falsity of $H$. Suppose it were discovered that there are two systems in us that produce overt actions, $S1$ and $S2$, that the systems never jointly produce an overt action, and that although intentions* or their physical correlates play a role in $S1$, they play no role in $S2$. Suppose further that $S2$ produces actions that almost all normal speakers of English count as intentional. Imagine, for example, that it is discovered that when we acquire proximal urges to $A$ (e.g., to say "Hi" to a friend one is walking past in the hallway) that are unopposed by other urges or thoughts, those proximal urges (or their physical correlates) directly activate the motoneurons to the relevant muscles: more specifically, they activate those motoneurons without generating any relevant intention and in the absence of any relevant intention. (When there is significant internal opposition, $S1$ is the operative system.) That discovery would persuade me that $H$ is false. (I leave working out the details of how such a discovery might be made as an exercise for the reader.) Of course, I have not insisted that $H$ is true. My thesis about $H$ is that the data Wegner marshals in support of his view do not warrant the claim that $H$ is false.

Regarding epiphenomenalism, Wegner writes:

> The experience of consciously willing an action ... serves as a kind of compass, alerting the conscious mind when actions occur that are likely to be the result of one's own agency.

The experience of will is therefore an indicator, one of those gauges on the control panel to which we refer as we steer. Like a compass reading, the feeling of doing tells us something about the operation of the ship. But also like a compass reading, this information must be understood as a conscious experience, a candidate for the dreaded "epiphenomenon" label. Just as compass readings do not steer the boat, conscious experiences of will do not cause human actions.

This chapter examines why the conscious experience of will might exist at all. Why, if this experience of will is not the cause of action, would we even go to the trouble of having it? What good is an epiphenomenon? (2002, pp. 317–18)

But why would anyone have thought that "the experience of consciously willing" an action that one performs is a cause of that action? Why wouldn't one instead have thought that "willing" (or consciously willing) an action (whatever, exactly, willing is supposed to be) is a cause of the action? My flipping a light switch—not my *experience* of flipping it— is a cause of a light going on. Why shouldn't we think, by analogy, that my acquiring a proximal intention to flip the switch—and not my experience of (acquiring) that intention, my "experience of consciously willing" to flip the switch, my "feeling" of flipping the switch, and so on—is a cause of my flipping it? When one is looking for causes of actions in strange places, finding an "epiphenomenon" there is not terribly surprising.

For my purposes, what is important in the present connection is whether proximal intentions* (or their physical correlates) play causal roles in the production of intentional actions—not, for example, whether Wegner is right or wrong in claiming that "the experience of consciously willing an action is not a direct indication that the conscious thought has caused the action" (2002, p. 2). Indeed, as I have explained, it is not clear what he means by this.[2]

I turn to intention acquisition. What might persuade me that all proximal intentions are acquired unconsciously?

Recall my strategy of silently saying "now!" to myself before flexing so as to have a relevant mental event to report in a Libet-style experiment. Perhaps I regarded my silently saying "now!" (in the imperative mood) as my way of consciously making a proximal decision to flex. But if I did, I might have been wrong about that. According to one relevant hypothesis, I unconsciously acquired a proximal intention to flex, I became aware of that intention some milliseconds later, and I misinterpreted becoming aware of it as consciously deciding to flex. In other words, my silently saying "now!" actually signified that I had become aware of my unconsciously acquired proximal intention to flex: I was in the grip of something in the ballpark of the illusion of conscious will. (This hypothesis about me may be generalized and refined to apply to all human agents and all of our conscious proximal intentions.)

How might the hypothesis about me be tested? Suppose we find that on average in my 40 trials, a type II RP began about 350 ms before I said "now!" Should we infer that, on average, I acquired a proximal intention to flex about 350 ms before I became conscious of it and said "now!"? No. As I explained in chapter 3, what is indicated by early stretches of the RP may be items in the preproximal intention group, potential *causes* of proximal intentions. Causes definitely should not be confused with their effects.

Suppose we locate a part of my brain (*B1*) that houses all and only the physical correlates of my proximal intentions* and a separate part of my brain (*B2*) that houses all and only the physical correlates of my conscious experiences. Suppose also that we find neural signatures for specific types of content—for example, a signature for the content "flex this wrist now," something that may be an aspect of the content of a proximal intention of mine and an aspect of the content of my conscious experience of such an intention.[3] Finally, suppose that in the experiment at issue, we find that activity with the "flex this wrist now" signature consistently occurs in *B1* about 50 ms before activity with that signature occurs in *B2* and that I consistently say "now!" shortly after that activity occurs in *B2*. That would persuade me that I acquire my proximal intentions to flex unconsciously and later become conscious of them. Of course, this imaginary evidence is just that—imaginary.

## 2. Free Will and Hypothetical Empirical Discoveries

What sort of empirical discovery would show that no one has free will? That depends on what "free will" means. Free will may be defined as the power to act freely (Mele 2006, p. 17). But what is meant by *act freely*? Familiar philosophical answers fall into two groups: compatibilist and incompatibilist. Compatibilism and incompatibilism are theses about the conceptual relationship between free action and determinism. *Determinism* is the thesis that a complete statement of the laws of nature together with a complete description of the condition of the entire universe at any point in time logically entails a complete description of the condition of the entire universe at any other point in time. *Compatibilism* is the thesis that free action is compatible with the truth of determinism. Because they attend to what contemporary physics tells us, the overwhelming majority of contemporary compatibilists do not believe that determinism is true, but they do believe that even if it were true, its truth would not entail that we never act freely. *Incompatibilism* is the thesis that free action is incompatible with the truth of determinism. In the incompatibilist group, most answers to the question what "free action" means come from libertarians. *Libertarianism* is the conjunction of incompatibilism and the thesis that some people sometimes act freely. Some incompatibilists argue that no one acts freely (Pereboom 2001;

Strawson 1986). They argue that even the falsity of determinism creates no place for free action.

I return to compatibilism, incompatibilism, and libertarianism shortly. A brief discussion of determinism will help minimize confusion. Some psychologists seem to disagree about the place of determinism in psychology. John Baer writes, "Determinism makes...psychology possible. If psychological events were not determined—caused—by antecedent events, psychology could make no sense" (2008, p. 309). George Howard agrees:

> If you want to be a scientist, you had better be a determinist. Things are (and act) the way they are (and act) because something (or some things) caused them to be (or act) that way. It is a proper job for a scientist to find and document (via experimental studies) the cause-effect relations that form and guide human actions. Therefore, I am a determinist. (2008, p. 261)

However, Roy Baumeister reports that he resents "being told that as a scientist" he is "required to embrace total causal determinism," and he remarks that determinism "is contrary to our data, which almost invariably show probabilistic rather than deterministic causation" (2008, p. 67). In a similar vein, Carol Dweck and Daniel Molden assert that "discovering predictability and lawfulness in human behavior does not imply determinism. We may measure certain personality factors and use our measures to predict people's behavior, but this does not mean that those factors...do not exert their influence in a probabilistic way" (2008, pp. 57–58).

Are Baer and Howard disagreeing with Baumeister, Dweck, and Molden, or are these two groups simply using the word "determinism" in two different ways? Suppose both groups were to agree to define "determinism" as I define it, and suppose another technical phrase—"psychological causalism"—were introduced and defined as the thesis that all psychological events, including overt and nonovert intentional actions, are caused, either deterministically or indeterministically (probabilistically). Would the apparent disagreement between the two groups dissolve? There is reason to think that it would. Notice that Baer equates "determined" with "caused." Howard seems to do the same in the passage I quoted. And, of course, psychological causalism is compatible with the idea that "If psychological events were not ... caused ... psychology could make no sense" (Baer 2008, p. 309). By "determinism" Baer and Howard might not mean anything more demanding than psychological causalism. And Baumeister, Dweck, and Molden give no indication that they would reject psychological causalism, though they do seem to reject determinism, as I define it.

Shaun Nichols (2008, p. 22) quotes the following from an article by John Bargh and Melissa Ferguson: "psychologists studying higher mental processes should continue the scientific study of conscious processes but at the same time give appropriate attention to the deterministic philosophy that must underlie such analysis" (2000, p. 940). Nichols adds, "psychological determinism has been and will continue to be a vital assumption guiding research. And I'm inclined to think it's true.... [M]y allegiance ... came from an abiding conviction that people's decisions *have* to have an explanation" (2008, p. 22). If what Nichols calls "psychological determinism" presupposes determinism (as I defined it), then there is no need for psychological determinism as a research-guiding assumption. What I called psychological causalism is easily paired with the idea that all decisions have causal explanations, given that not all adequate causal explanations require deterministic causes to be at work. Whether decisions and other interesting events are *deterministically* caused is an empirical issue. Psychological causalism is a sufficiently strong assumption for psychologists to proceed on.

Dweck and Molden raise a question about how laws of nature are understood in a standard philosophical definition of "determinism" (2008, p. 45). Do "laws of human nature" count? What Albert Bandura calls "epistemological reductionism" is relevant here (2008, p. 110). It "contends that the laws governing higher level psychosocial phenomena are ultimately reducible to the laws operating at the atomic and molecular levels." *If* the laws of physics are permanently in place shortly after the Big Bang, then *if* the universe is deterministic and devoid of nonphysical entities, it would seem that all that is needed for entailments of all future events and regularities is in place long before there are any living beings at all. Given these assumptions, the laws (regularities) of human nature would seem to be entailed by a complete description of the laws of physics and of the condition of the universe long before the advent of human beings. This upshot resembles the reductionism that Bandura has in mind. If the universe is not deterministic, the combination of the laws at the level of physics and the state of the universe at a given early time may leave it open to a significant extent what the psychological laws (regularities) will be.

I should add that to say that a universe is not deterministic (or indeterministic), as I use these terms, is just to say that determinism is not true of that universe. It certainly is not to say that psychological causalism is false of it.

Compatibilism, again, is the thesis that free action is compatible with the truth of determinism. This thesis usually sounds strange to nonspecialists. When people first encounter the pair of expressions "free will" and "determinism," they tend to get the impression that the two ideas are defined in opposition to each other, that they are mutually exclusive by definition. This is one reason that it is useful to think of free will as the power to act freely and regard acting freely as the more basic notion—that is, as a notion in terms of which free will is to be defined. Consider the following conversation between two police officers who have a notoriously stingy friend named Stan.

> Ann: Stan gave $20 to a homeless man today.
> Bill: Why? Did he hold a gun to Stan's head?
> Ann: No, Stan freely gave him the money.

Surely, Ann and Bill do not need to have an opinion about whether determinism (as defined above) is true to have this conversation. If what Ann says is true—that is, if Stan freely gave away $20—and free will is the power to act freely, then Stan has free will (or had it at that time). Even if "free will" is typically opposed to "determinism" in ordinary speech, "he freely did it" seems not to be. And even if "he freely did it" were typically opposed to "determinism" in ordinary speech, that would settle nothing. After all, in ordinary speech, deductive reasoning seems to be defined as reasoning from the general to the particular, and that certainly would only jokingly be said to constitute an objection to a logician's definition of deduction (according to which "Ann is a police officer; Bill is a police officer; therefore Ann and Bill are police officers" is a valid deductive argument).

Compatibilist theories of free action emphasize a distinction between deterministic causation and compulsion.[4] If determinism is true, then my eating a banana for breakfast today and my working on this chapter today were deterministically caused; so were a certain compulsive hand-washer's washing his hands dozens of times today, a certain delusional person's spending the day trying to contact God with his microwave oven, a certain addict's using his favorite drug while in the grip of an irresistible urge to do so, and a certain person's handing over money to gunmen who convincingly threatened to kill him if he refused. But there is an apparent difference. I am sane and free from addiction, and I received no death threats today. The basic compatibilist idea is (roughly) that when mentally healthy people act intentionally and rationally in the absence of compulsion and coercion they act freely, and an action's being deterministically caused does not suffice for its being compelled or coerced.[5]

Many compatibilists have been concerned to accommodate the idea that, for example, if I freely spent the day working, I could have done something else instead. They grant that if determinism is true, then there is a sense in which people could never have done otherwise than they did: they could not have done otherwise in the sense that their doing otherwise is inconsistent with the combination of the past and the laws of nature. But, these compatibilists say, the fact that a person never could have done otherwise in that sense is irrelevant to free action. What is relevant is that people who act freely are exercising a rational capacity of such a kind that if their situation had been different in any one of a variety of important ways, they would have responded to the difference with a different suitable action (Smith 2003). For example, although I spent the day working, I would have spent the day relaxing if someone had bet me $500 that I would not relax all day. This truth is consistent with determinism. (Notice that if someone had made this bet with me, the past would have been different from what it actually was.) And it reinforces the distinction between deterministic causation and compulsion. Offer a compulsive hand-washer $500 not to wash his hands all day and see what happens.

Like compatibilists, some libertarians maintain that when mentally healthy people act intentionally in the absence of compulsion and coercion they act freely, but libertarians insist that the deterministic causation of an action is incompatible with the action's being freely performed. Some libertarian theories of free action assert that agents never act freely unless some of their actions are indeterministically caused by immediate antecedents (Kane 1996). Whereas the laws of nature that apply to deterministic causation are exceptionless, those that apply most directly to indeterministic causation are instead probabilistic.[6] Typically, events like *deciding* to help a stranded motorist—as distinct from the overt actions involved in actually helping—are counted as mental actions. Suppose that Ann's decision to help a stranded motorist is indeterministically caused by (among other things) her thinking that she should help. Because the causation is indeterministic, she might not have decided to help given exactly the same internal and external conditions. Some libertarians appeal to indeterministic causation to secure the possibility of doing otherwise that they require for free action.

According to typical event-causal libertarian views (and to an integrated agent-causal libertarian view), the *proximate* causes of directly free actions indeterministically cause them.[7] This is a consequence of the typical event-causal (and integrated agent-causal) libertarian ideas that free actions have proximate causes and that in basic cases of free action, if an agent freely *A*-s at *t* in world *W*, he does not *A* at *t* in some other possible world with the same laws of nature and the same past up to *t*. Now the proximate causes of actions, including actions that are decisions, are internal to agents. Even a driver's sudden decision to hit the brakes in an emergency situation is not proximately caused by events in the external world. Perception of whatever the source of the emergency happens to be—for example, a dog running into traffic—is causally involved. And how the driver decides to react to what he sees depends on, among other things, his driving skills and habits, whether he is aware of what is happening directly behind him, and his preferences. A driver who likes driving over dogs and is always looking for opportunities to do so would probably react very differently than a normal person would. In light of the general point about the proximate causation of actions, typical event-causal (and integrated agent-causal) libertarianism encompasses a commitment to what may be called *agent-internal indeterminism*.[8]

What libertarians want that determinism precludes is not merely that agents have open to them more than one future that is compatible with the combination of the past and the laws of nature, but also that, on some occasions, which possible future becomes actual is in some sense and to some degree up to the agents. They want something that seemingly requires that agents themselves be indeterministic in some suitable way—that some relevant things that happen under the skin are indeterministically caused by other such things. The focus is on psychological events (or their physical correlates), as opposed, for example, to indeterministically caused muscle spasms—and, more specifically, on psychological events that have a significant bearing on action (or the physical correlates of these events).

Many distinct libertarian and compatibilist theories about the nature of free will are in circulation. All of them have been challenged. Reviewing the major details of the debates is well beyond the scope of this book. My aim thus far in the section has been to provide a theoretical context for the question with which I opened it: what sort of empirical discovery would show that no one has free will?

Start with libertarian views of the sort I have described. Quantum mechanics, according to leading interpretations, is indeterministic. But indeterminism at that level does not ensure that any human brains themselves sometimes operate indeterministically (that is, that some causal processes that happen entirely within the brain are indeterministic), much less that they sometimes operate indeterministically in ways appropriate for free action. One possibility, as David Hodgson reports, is that "in systems as hot, wet, and massive as neurons of the brain, quantum mechanical indeterminacies quickly cancel out, so that for all practical purposes determinism rules in the brain" (2002, p. 86). Another is that any indeterminism in the human brain is simply irrelevant to the production of actions. Empirical discoveries that either of these possibilities is an actuality would show that we do not have free will on some familiar libertarian conceptions of free will.

Compatibilist conceptions of free will do not require indeterminism. The hypothetical empirical discoveries just mentioned pose no threat to free will as compatibilists conceive of it. What kinds of empirical discovery would show that we never act freely, even assuming the truth of compatibilism? The discovery that all of our thoughts and behavior are produced by fancy machines controlled by intelligent inhabitants of another galaxy would do.[9] But, of course, this is far-fetched. What about something much closer to home?

Wegner asserts, "The mind...really doesn't *know* what causes its own actions. Whatever empirical will there is rumbling along in the engine room...might in fact be totally inscrutable to the driver of the machine (the mind).... The mind can't ever know itself well enough to be able to say what the causes of its actions are" (2002, p. 28); and he proceeds to quote Marvin Minsky's suggestion (1985, p. 306) that our decisions are "determined by internal forces [that we] do not understand." Take a step beyond these thoughts and consider the hypothetical discovery that we are always radically mistaken about why we are doing what we are doing—not because of the highjinks of extraterrestrials, but because the conceptual scheme that we use to interpret and explain our behavior always radically misleads us. Suppose it were discovered that what we regard as intentions, beliefs, and desires, along with their physical correlates, have nothing at all to do with the production of any of our behavior and that all of our behavior is produced entirely by hidden sources that only highly trained scientists have even a ghost of a chance of understanding.[10] That would seem to show that we have never acted freely, even on compatibilist conceptions. Of course, Wegner does not provide grounds for believing that this hypothetical discovery will ever be made.

I hope it is clear that I am not suggesting that *only* the imaginary empirical discoveries just described would convince me that we never act freely. Other empirical discoveries might do so as well. (And some empirical discoveries may imply that free action is not as common as many people think.) Similarly, I was not suggesting in section 1 that only the imaginary empirical discoveries discussed there would show that hypothesis *H* is false or that all proximal intentions are acquired unconsciously.

## 3. Parting Remarks

Human action long ago captured the attention of philosophers and scientists. Early in chapter 1, I mentioned the dismissive attitude that some members of each group take toward the other group's work on this topic, and I said that one moral of this book would be that this dismissiveness is a mistake—on each side. I have been more critical here of claims made by scientists than of claims made by philosophers, but that fact is explained by what this book is and is not. It is not an attempt at even-handed criticism of work on human action in various fields; it is in part an attempt to show that some recent bold claims about human action are unwarranted—claims that, in the words of Pockett, Banks, and Gallagher, have "seized the philosophical and scientific imagination and again brought the whole question [whether 'consciousness causes behavior'] to the forefront of intellectual debate" (2006, p. 1). To some extent in this book, and to a greater extent in some other books (Mele 1987, 1992, 1995, 2001b, 2003), I have made positive use of good scientific work in an effort to understand aspects of human behavior. (My treatment of an intriguing issue about self-control in chapter 8 of Mele 2003 benefits significantly from Libet's work.) I closed *Motivation and Agency* with the assertion that a traditional philosophical approach to human action that dates back to Plato and Aristotle "has a firm basis of support in the human sciences, and the potential for mutual intellectual benefit is enormous" (Mele 2003, p. 244), and I definitely continue to believe that.

Another moral of this book, I hope, is that good conceptual work is useful in producing a theoretical context that sheds considerable light on data. Such work can significantly raise the probability that we avoid seriously misinterpreting data, and it can do the same for the avoidance of seriously faulty inferences from our data.

In chapter 5, I quoted the following passage from Dennett (2003) to pave the way for the truism that if one sets the bar for the existence of free will or anything else ridiculously high, the assertion that it exists should strike one as ridiculous:

> If you are one of those who think that free will is only *really* free will if it springs from an immaterial soul that hovers happily in your brain, shooting arrows of decision into your motor cortex, then, given what *you* mean by free will, my view is that there is no free will at all. If, on the other hand, you think free will might be morally important without being supernatural, then my view is that free will is indeed real, but just not quite what you probably thought it was. (p. 222)

Although Dennett and I do not see entirely eye to eye about free will (see Dennett 2003 on Mele 1995, and Mele 2005 on Dennett 2003), I certainly agree with him that the only sensible place to look for it is in the natural order. This is also the only sensible place to look for "conscious will"—or, as I would prefer to say, conscious decisions and intentions. Conceived of as essentially supernatural, effective intentions and decisions and the power of conscious will have a ghost of a chance—or, more aptly, a ghost's chance—of existing. Conceived of more naturally, their being every bit as real as you and I are is consistent with the scientific findings examined in this book.

In my preface, I quoted an e-mail message from someone who was upset by the news that neuroscientists had shown that free will is an illusion. She was, she said, "in a lot of despair." My final moral is the title of a song: "Don't Worry, Be Happy." Scientists have not shown this. Nor has anyone shown that there are no effective intentions. This is good news for just about everyone.

### NOTES

1. For an excellent brief critical review of various relevant philosophical positions that highlights the metaphysical nature of the debate, see Jackson (2000).

2. If by "the experience of consciously willing an action" Wegner means something like "a conscious intention to *A*" or "consciously deciding to *A*," then he is looking for causes of actions in an intuitively more reasonable place. But as I argued in chapter 7, there is powerful evidence that conscious decisions and intentions sometimes are among the causes of corresponding intentional actions.

3. For a discussion of some evidence that specific types of content have "brain-wave" signatures, see Suppes (2002, pp. 452–54).

4. See Audi (1993, chaps. 7 and 10); Ayer (1954); Frankfurt (1988); Grünbaum (1971); Mill (1979, chap. 26, esp. pp. 464–67); Schlick (1962, chap. 7); and Smith (2003). Also see Hume's remarks on the liberty of spontaneity versus the liberty of indifference (1739, bk. II, pt. III, sec. 2).

5. Notice that the condition just offered is an alleged sufficient condition for free action, not an alleged set of individually necessary and jointly sufficient conditions.

6. So if the occurrence of $x$ (at time $t1$) indeterministically causes the occurrence of $y$ (at $t2$), then a complete description of the universe at $t1$ together with a complete statement of the laws of nature does *not* entail that $y$ occurs at $t2$. There

was at most a high probability that the occurrence of $x$ at $t1$ would cause the occurrence of $y$ at $t2$.

7.  Randolph Clarke's "integrated agent-causal account [of free will] takes the exercise of freedom-level active control to consist in causation of an action by mental events and by the agent" (2003, p. 178). The causation at issue is not deterministic: the integrated agent-causal view is a libertarian view. The view is carefully developed in Clarke (2003). For critical discussion, see Mele (2006, chap. 3).

8.  In this paragraph and the next one, I borrow from Mele (2006, pp. 9–10).

9.  Of course, people can say whatever they like, and some compatibilists may say that even the imagined discovery is compatible with our acting freely. This is not the place to discuss this issue. On compatibilism, see Mele (2006, chaps. 6–8).

10.  It may be objected that if functionalism is true, this discovery is conceptually impossible—that by definition, types of mental state cut off in the imagined way from behavior do not qualify as *intention, belief,* or *desire*. But "what we regard as intentions, beliefs, and desires" (to quote from the sentence to which this note is appended) might not exist. If eliminativists are right, they do not exist.

# References

Adams, F., and A. Mele. 1992. "The Intention/Volition Debate." *Canadian Journal of Philosophy* 22: 323–38.

Andersen, R., and C. Buneo. 2002. "Intentional Maps in Posterior Parietal Cortex." *Annual Review of Neuroscience* 25: 189–220.

Astington, J., and A. Gopnik. 1991. "Understanding Desire and Intention." In A. Whiten, ed., *Natural Theories of Mind: The Evolution, Development and Simulation of Second-Order Representations.* Oxford: Basil Blackwell.

Audi, R. 1993. *Action, Intention, and Reason.* Ithaca, N.Y.: Cornell University Press.

Ayer, A. 1954. "Freedom and Necessity." In *Philosophical Essays.* London: Macmillan.

Baer, J. 2008. "Free Will Requires Determinism." In J. Baer, J. Kaufman, and R. Baumeister, eds. *Are We Free? Psychology and Free Will.* New York: Oxford University Press.

Bandura, A. 2008. "Reconstrual of 'Free Will' from the Agentic Perspective of Social Cognitive Theory." In J. Baer, J. Kaufman, and R. Baumeister, eds. *Are We Free? Psychology and Free Will.* New York: Oxford University Press.

Banks, W. 2006. "Does Consciousness Cause Misbehavior?" In S. Pockett, W. Banks, and S. Gallagher, eds. *Does Consciousness Cause Behavior? An Investigation of the Nature of Volition.* Cambridge, Mass.: MIT Press.

Bargh, J., and T. Chartrand. 1999. "The Unbearable Automaticity of Being." *American Psychologist* 54: 462–79.

Bargh, J., and M. Ferguson. 2000. "Beyond Behaviorism: On the Automaticity of Higher Mental Processes." *Psychological Bulletin* 126: 925–45.

Baumeister, R. 2008. "Free Will, Consciousness, and Cultural Animals." In J. Baer, J. Kaufman, and R. Baumeister, eds. *Are We Free? Psychology and Free Will.* New York: Oxford University Press.

Bayne, T. 2006. "Phenomenology and the Feeling of Doing." In S. Pockett, W. Banks, and S. Gallagher, eds. *Does Consciousness Cause Behavior? An Investigation of the Nature of Volition.* Cambridge, Mass.: MIT Press.

Brand, M. 1984. *Intending and Acting.* Cambridge, Mass.: MIT Press.

Brass, M., and P. Haggard. 2007. "To Do or Not to Do: The Neural Signature of Self-Control." *Journal of Neuroscience* 27: 9141–45.

Bratman, M. 1987. *Intention, Plans, and Practical Reason.* Cambridge, Mass.: Harvard University Press.

Breitmeyer, B. 1985. "Problems with the Psychophysics of Intention." *Behavioral and Brain Sciences* 8: 539–40.

Cacioppo, J., and R. Petty. 1981. "Electromyographic Specificity during Covert Information Processing." *Psychophysiology* 18: 518–23.

Caldara, R., M. Deiber, C. Andrey, C. Michel, et al. 2004. "Actual and Mental Motor Preparation and Execution: A Spatiotemporal ERP Study." *Experimental Brain Research* 159: 389–99.

Campbell, C. 1957. *On Selfhood and Godhood.* London: Allen and Unwin.

Campbell, J., M. O'Rourke, and H. Silverstein, eds. In press. *Action, Ethics, and Responsibility* Cambridge, Mass: MIT Press.

Carruthers, P. 2007. "The Illusion of Conscious Will." *Synthese* 159: 197–213.

Clarke, R. 2003. *Libertarian Accounts of Free Will.* Oxford: Oxford University Press.

Davidson, D. 1980. *Essays on Actions and Events.* Oxford: Clarendon Press.

Day, B., J. Rothwell, P. Thompson, A. Maertens de Noordhout, K. Nakashima, K. Shannon, and C. Marsden. 1989. "Delay in the Execution of Voluntary Movement by Electrical or Magnetic Brain Stimulation in Intact Man." *Brain* 112: 649–63.

Dennett, D. 2003. *Freedom Evolves.* New York: Viking.

Dweck, C., and D. Molden. 2008. "Self-Theories: The Construction of Free Will." In J. Baer, J. Kaufman, and R. Baumeister, eds. *Are*

*We Free? Psychology and Free Will*. New York: Oxford University Press.

Ehrsson, H., S. Geyer, and E. Naito. 2003. "Imagery of Voluntary Movement of Fingers, Toes, and Tongue Activates Corresponding Body-Part-Specific Motor Representations." *Journal of Neurophysiology* 90: 3304–16.

Fischer, J., and M. Ravizza. 1992. "When the Will Is Free." *Philosophical Perspectives* 6: 423–51.

Fisher, C. 2001. "If There Were No Free Will." *Medical Hypotheses* 56: 364–66.

Frankfurt, H. 1988. *The Importance of What We Care About*. Cambridge: Cambridge University Press.

Ginet, C. 1990. *On Action*. Cambridge: Cambridge University Press.

Goldman, A. 1970. *A Theory of Human Action*. Englewood Cliffs, N.J.: Prentice Hall.

Gollwitzer, P. 1993. "Goal Achievement: The Role of Intentions." *European Review of Social Psychology* 4: 141–85.

———1996. "The Volitional Benefits of Planning." In P. Gollwitzer and J. Bargh, eds., *The Psychology of Action*. New York: Guilford.

———1999. "Implementation Intentions." *American Psychologist* 54: 493–503.

Gollwitzer, P., and P. Sheeran. 2006. "Implementation Intentions and Goal Achievement: A Meta-Analysis of Effects and Processes." *Advances in Experimental Social Psychology* 38: 69–119.

Gomes, G. 1999. "Volition and the Readiness Potential." *Journal of Consciousness Studies* 6: 59–76.

Grünbaum, A. 1971. "Free Will and the Laws of Human Behavior." *American Philosophical Quarterly* 8: 299–317.

Haggard, P. 2005. "Conscious Intention and Motor Cognition." *Trends in Cognitive Sciences* 9: 290–95.

———2006. "Conscious Intention and the Sense of Agency." In N. Sebanz and W. Prinz, eds., *Disorders of Volition*. Cambridge, Mass.: MIT Press.

Haggard, P., and S. Clark. 2003. "Intentional Action: Conscious Experience and Neural Prediction." *Consciousness and Cognition* 12: 695–707.

Haggard, P., and M. Eimer. 1999. "On the Relation between Brain Potentials and the Awareness of Voluntary Movements." *Experimental Brain Research* 126: 128–33.

Haggard, P., and B. Libet. 2001. "Conscious Intention and Brain Activity." *Journal of Consciousness Studies* 8: 47–63.

Haggard, P., and E. Magno. 1999. "Localising Awareness of Action with Transcranial Magnetic Stimulation." *Experimental Brain Research* 127: 102–7.

Haggard, P., C. Newman, and E. Magno. 1999. "On the Perceived Time of Voluntary Actions." *British Journal of Psychology* 90: 291–303.

Hallett, M. 2007. "Volitional Control of Movement: The Physiology of Free Will." *Clinical Neurophysiology* 118: 1179–92.

Hardcastle, V. 2004. "The Elusive Illusion of Sensation." *Behavioral and Brain Sciences* 27: 662–63.

Harman, G. 1976. "Practical Reasoning." *Review of Metaphysics* 79: 431–63.

——— 1986. *Change in View*. Cambridge, Mass.: MIT Press.

Hodgson, D. 2002. "Quantum Physics, Consciousness, and Free Will." In R. Kane, ed., *The Oxford Handbook of Free Will*. New York: Oxford University Press.

Holton, R. 2004. "Review of *The Illusion of Conscious Will* by Daniel Wegner." *Mind* 113: 218–21.

Howard, G. 2008. "Whose Will? How Free?" In J. Baer, J. Kaufman, and R. Baumeister, eds. *Are We Free? Psychology and Free Will*. New York: Oxford University Press.

Hume, D. 1739. *A Treatise of Human Nature*. Reprinted in L. Selby-Bigge, ed., *A Treatise of Human Nature*. Oxford: Clarendon Press, 1975.

Jackson, F. 2000. "Psychological Explanation and Implicit Theory." *Philosophical Explorations* 3: 83–95.

Jahanshahi, M., I. Jenkins, R. Brown, C. Marsden, R. Passingham, and D. Brooks. 1995. "Self-Initiated versus Externally Triggered Movements." *Brain* 118: 913–33.

James, W. 1890. *The Principles of Psychology*, vol. 2. Cambridge, Mass.: Harvard University Press.

Jankelowitz, S., and J. Colebatch. 2002. "Movement Related Potentials Associated with Self-Paced, Cued and Imagined Arm Movements." *Experimental Brain Research* 147: 98–107.

Jorgensen, C., and K. Binsted. 2005. "Web Browser Control Using EMG Based Subvocal Speech Recognition." *Proceedings of the 38th Hawaii International Conference on System Sciences* 38: 1–8.

Kane, R. 1989. "Two Kinds of Incompatibilism." *Philosophy and Phenomenological Research* 50: 219–54.

——— 1996. *The Significance of Free Will.* New York: Oxford University Press.

Keller, I., and H. Heckhausen. 1990. "Readiness Potentials Preceding Spontaneous Motor Acts: Voluntary vs. Involuntary Control." *Electroencephalography and Clinical Neurophysiology* 76: 351–61.

Kilner, J., C. Vargas, S. Duval, S. Blakemore, and A. Sirigu. 2004. "Motor Activation Prior to Observation of a Predicted Movement." *Nature Neuroscience* 7: 1299–301.

Kim, J. 2003. "Supervenience, Emergence, Realization, Reduction." In M. Loux and D. Zimmerman, eds. *Oxford Handbook of Metaphysics.* Oxford: Clarendon Press.

Lau, H., R. Rogers, and R. Passingham. 2007. "Manipulating the Experienced Onset of Intention after Action Execution." *Journal of Cognitive Neuroscience* 19: 81–90.

Lau, H., R. Rogers, N. Ramnani, and R. Passingham. 2004. "Willed Action and Attention to the Selection of Action." *Neuroimage* 21: 1407–14.

Lhermitte, F. 1983. "Utilization Behavior and Its Relation to Lesions of the Frontal Lobes." *Brain* 106: 237–55.

——— 1986. "Human Autonomy and the Frontal Lobes." *Annals of Neurology* 19: 335–43.

Libet, B. 1985. "Unconscious Cerebral Initiative and the Role of Conscious Will in Voluntary Action." *Behavioral and Brain Sciences* 8: 529–66.

——— 1989. "The Timing of a Subjective Experience." *Behavioral and Brain Sciences* 12: 183–84.

——— 1992. "The Neural Time-Factor in Perception, Volition and Free Will." *Revue de Métaphysique et de Morale* 2: 255–72.

——— 1999. "Do We Have Free Will?" *Journal of Consciousness Studies* 6: 47–57.

——— 2001. "Consciousness, Free Action and the Brain." *Journal of Consciousness Studies* 8: 59–65.

——— 2002. "The Timing of Mental Events: Libet's Experimental Findings and Their Implications." *Consciousness and Cognition* 11: 291–99.

——— 2004. *Mind Time*. Cambridge, Mass.: Harvard University Press.

Libet, B., C. Gleason, E. Wright, and D. Pearl. 1983. "Time of Unconscious Intention to Act in Relation to Onset of Cerebral Activity (Readiness-Potential)." *Brain* 106: 623–42.

Libet, B., E. Wright, and A. Curtis. 1983. "Preparation- or Intention-to-Act, in Relation to Pre-Event Potentials Recorded at the Vertex." *Electroencephalography and Clinical Neurophysiology* 56: 367–72.

Libet, B., E. Wright, and C. Gleason. 1982. "Readiness Potentials Preceding Unrestricted 'Spontaneous' vs. Pre-Planned Voluntary Acts." *Electroencephalography and Clinical Neurophysiology* 54: 322–35.

Logan, G. 1994. "On the Ability to Inhibit Thought and Action: A Users' Guide to the Stop Signal Paradigm." In E. Dagenbach and T. Carr, eds., *Inhibitory Processes in Attention, Memory, and Language*. San Diego: Academic Press.

Marcel, A. 2003. "The Sense of Agency: Awareness and Ownership of Action." In J. Roessler and N. Eilan, eds., *Agency and Self-Awareness*. Oxford: Clarendon Press.

Marchetti, C., and S. Della Salla. 1998. "Disentangling the Alien and Anarchic Hand." *Cognitive Neuropsychiatry* 3: 191–207.

McCann, H. 1986. "Intrinsic Intentionality." *Theory and Decision* 20: 247–73.

Mele, A. 1987. *Irrationality*. New York: Oxford University Press.

——— 1992. *Springs of Action*. New York: Oxford University Press.

——— 1995. *Autonomous Agents*. New York: Oxford University Press.

——— 1997. "Strength of Motivation and Being in Control: Learning from Libet." *American Philosophical Quarterly* 34: 319–32.

——— 2001a. "Acting Intentionally: Probing Folk Notions," in B. Malle, L. Moses, and D. Baldwin, eds., *Intentions and Intentionality: Foundations of Social Cognition*. Cambridge, Mass.: MIT Press.

———— 2001b. *Self-Deception Unmasked*. Princeton, N.J.: Princeton University Press.

———— 2003. *Motivation and Agency*. New York: Oxford University Press.

———— 2004. "The Illusion of Conscious Will and the Causation of Intentional Actions." *Philosophical Topics* 32: 193–213.

———— 2005. "Dennett on Freedom." *Metaphilosophy* 36: 414–26.

———— 2006. *Free Will and Luck*. New York: Oxford University Press.

———— 2007. "Persisting Intentions." *Noûs* 41: 735–57.

———— 2008a. "Proximal Intentions, Intention-Reports, and Vetoing." *Philosophical Psychology* 21: 1–14.

———— 2008b. "Psychology and Free Will: A Commentary." In J. Baer, J. Kaufman, and R. Baumeister, eds., *Are We Free? Psychology and Free Will*. New York: Oxford University Press.

———— 2008c. "Recent Work on Free Will and Science." *American Philosophical Quarterly* 45: 107–29.

Mele, A., and S. Sverdlik. 1996. "Intention, Intentional Action, and Moral Responsibility." *Philosophical Studies* 82: 265–87.

Mill, J. S. 1979. *An Examination of Sir William Hamilton's Philosophy*. J. Robson, ed. Toronto: Routledge and Kegan Paul.

Minsky, M. 1985. *The Society of Mind*. New York: Simon and Schuster.

Musallam, S., B. Corneil, B. Greger, H. Scherberger, and R. Andersen. 2004. "Cognitive Control Signals for Neural Prosthetics." *Science* 305: 258–62.

Näätänen, R. 1985. "Brain Physiology and the Unconscious Initiation of Movements." *Behavioral and Brain Sciences* 8: 549.

Nahmias, E. 2002. "When Consciousness Matters: A Critical Review of Daniel Wegner's *The Illusion of Conscious Will*." *Philosophical Psychology* 15: 527–41.

Nichols, S. 2008. "How Can Psychology Contribute to the Free Will Debate?" In J. Baer, J. Kaufman, and R. Baumeister, eds., *Are We Free? Psychology and Free Will*. New York: Oxford University Press.

O'Connor, T. 2000. *Persons and Causes*. New York: Oxford University Press.

O'Shaughnessy, B. 1980. *The Will*, vol. 2. Cambridge: Cambridge University Press.

Pacherie, E. 2006. "Toward a Dynamic Theory of Intentions." In S. Pockett, W. Banks, and S. Gallagher, eds., *Does Consciousness Cause Behavior? An Investigation of the Nature of Volition*. Cambridge, Mass.: MIT Press.

Passingham, R., and H. Lau. 2006. "Free Choice and the Human Brain." In S. Pockett, W. Banks, and S. Gallagher, eds., *Does Consciousness Cause Behavior? An Investigation of the Nature of Volition*. Cambridge, Mass.: MIT Press.

Peacocke, C. 1985. "Intention and Akrasia." In B. Vermazen and M. Hintikka, eds., *Essays on Davidson*. Oxford: Clarendon Press.

Pereboom, D. 2001. *Living without Free Will*. Cambridge: Cambridge University Press.

Pink, T. 1996. *The Psychology of Freedom*. Cambridge: Cambridge University Press.

Pockett, S. 2006. "The Neuroscience of Movement." In S. Pockett, W. Banks, and S. Gallagher, eds., *Does Consciousness Cause Behavior? An Investigation of the Nature of Volition*. Cambridge, Mass.: MIT Press.

Pockett, S., W. Banks, and S. Gallagher, eds. 2006. *Does Consciousness Cause Behavior? An Investigation of the Nature of Volition*. Cambridge, Mass.: MIT Press.

Prinz, W. 2003. "How Do We Know about Our Own Actions?" In S. Maasen, W. Prinz, and G. Roth, eds., *Voluntary Action*. Oxford: Oxford University Press.

Ramachandran, V. 2004. *A Brief Tour of Human Consciousness*. New York: Pi Press.

Roediger, H., M. Goode, and F. Zaromb. 2008. "Free Will and the Control of Action." In J. Baer, J. Kaufman, and R. Baumeister, eds., *Are We Free? Psychology and Free Will*. New York: Oxford University Press.

Schlick, M. 1962. *Problems of Ethics*. David Rynin, trans. New York: Dover.

Searle, J. 1983. *Intentionality*. Cambridge: Cambridge University Press.

———— 2001. *Rationality in Action*. Cambridge, Mass.: MIT Press.

Shariff, A., J. Schooler, and K. Vohs. 2008. "The Hazards of Claiming to Have Solved the Hard Problem of Free Will." In J. Baer,

J. Kaufman, and R. Baumeister, eds., *Are We Free? Psychology and Free Will*. New York: Oxford University Press.

Smith, M. 2003. "Rational Capacities, or: How to Distinguish Recklessness, Weakness, and Compulsion." In S. Stroud and C. Tappolet, eds., *Weakness of Will and Practical Irrationality*. Oxford: Clarendon Press.

Spence, S., and C. Frith. 1999. "Towards a Functional Anatomy of Volition." *Journal of Consciousness Studies* 6: 11–29.

Strawson, G. 1986. *Freedom and Belief*. Oxford: Clarendon Press.

Suppes, P. 2002. *Representation and Invariance of Scientific Structures*. Stanford, Calif.: CSLI Publications.

Toates, F. 2006. "A Model of the Hierarchy of Behaviour, Cognition, and Consciousness." *Consciousness and Cognition* 15: 75–118.

Ullmann-Margalit, E., and S. Morgenbesser. 1977. "Picking and Choosing." *Social Research* 44: 757–85.

van de Grind, W. 2002. "Physical, Neural, and Mental Timing." *Consciousness and Cognition* 11: 241–64.

van Inwagen, P. 1989. "When Is the Will Free?" *Philosophical Perspectives* 3: 399–422.

Vohs, K., and J. Schooler. 2008. "The Value of Believing in Free Will: Encouraging a Belief in Determinism Increases Cheating." *Psychological Science* 19: 49–54.

Wegner, D. 2002. *The Illusion of Conscious Will*. Cambridge, Mass.: MIT Press.

——— 2004a. "Frequently Asked Questions about Conscious Will." *Behavioral and Brain Sciences* 27: 679–88.

——— 2004b. "Précis of *The Illusion of Conscious Will*." *Behavioral and Brain Sciences* 27: 649–59.

——— 2008. "Self Is Magic." In J. Baer, J. Kaufman, and R. Baumeister, eds., *Are We Free? Psychology and Free Will*. New York: Oxford University Press.

Zhu, J. 2003. "Reclaiming Volition." *Consciousness and Cognition* 10: 61–77.

Zimmerman, D. 2006. "Dualism in the Philosophy of Mind." In D. Borchert, ed., *Encyclopedia of Philosophy*, 2nd ed. Detroit: Thomson Gale, vol. 3, pp. 113–22.

# Index